# Mad Hatter

## A season on 2 wheels - 2021/22

**Mark Crowther**
**Foreward by Mick Harford**

Published by New Generation Publishing in 2022

Copyright © Mark Crowther 2022

First Edition

The author asserts the moral right under the Copyright, Designs and Patents Act 1988 to be identified as the author of this work.

All Rights reserved. No part of this publication may be reproduced, stored in a retrieval system or transmitted, in any form or by any means without the prior consent of the author, nor be otherwise circulated in any form of binding or cover other than that which it is published and without a similar condition being imposed on the subsequent purchaser.

ISBN: 978-1-80369-666-9

www.newgeneration-publishing.com

New Generation Publishing

# Contents

Foreword By Mick Harford .................................................................. 1
INTRODUCTION ................................................................................. 3
40 years of ups and downs following the Hatters ............................. 5
My struggles with my mental health .................................................. 10
Season 2020/2021 – COVID-19 and Watford rivalry resumed ...... 16
My Mad Hatter Away Cycle Challenge ............................................ 20
Tuesday 10th August 21 – Stevenage Borough ............................... 24
Saturday 14th August 21 – West Bromwich Albion ....................... 28
Tuesday 17th August 21 - Barnsley .................................................. 31
Mainstream media interest ................................................................. 35
Saturday 11th September 21 – Blackburn Rovers .......................... 37
Wednesday 15th September 21 – Bristol City ................................. 41
Saturday 25th September 21 - Bournemouth .................................. 44
Saturday 16th October 21 - Millwall ................................................ 47
Tuesday 19th October 21 – Derby County ...................................... 50
Saturday 30th October 21 – Preston North End ............................. 53
Friday 19th November 21 – Queens Park Rangers ........................ 58
Tuesday 23rd November 21 – Nottingham Forest .......................... 62
Saturday 4th December 21 - Blackpool ........................................... 65
COVID-19 and a month without football ........................................ 71
Wednesday 19th January 22 - Reading ............................................ 73
Saturday 22nd January 22 – Sheffield United ................................. 76
Tuesday 1st February 22 – Swansea City ........................................ 81
Saturday 5th February 22 – Cambridge United .............................. 89

Saturday 12th February 22 – Birmingham City .............................. 92

Wednesday 23rd February 22 – Stoke City ...................................... 96

Saturday 5th March 22 - Middlesbrough......................................... 99

Tuesday 8th March 22 – Coventry City ......................................... 106

COVID-19 & postponed cycle challenge to Hull City ................. 109

Saturday 26th & Sunday 27th March 22 – Hull City ..................... 111

Tuesday 5th April 22 – Peterborough United................................. 115

Monday 11th April 22 – Huddersfield Town ................................. 119

Monday 18th April 22 – Cardiff City ............................................. 124

Sunday 24th April 22 – EFL Awards ............................................. 128

Monday 2nd May 22 - Fulham ....................................................... 133

A celebration of the season's achievements .................................. 138

Monday 16th May 22 – Huddersfield Town .................................. 144

Mad Hatter Away Cycle Challenge Achieved............................... 150

# Foreword By Mick Harford

I'd like to start by saying what an honour it is for me to be asked by Mark to write the foreword for this book.

Mark has been an inspiration for me in my battle with prostate cancer over the past couple of years, and I'm so glad that he managed to raise so much money and awareness for three great charities in Prostate Cancer UK, Keech House Hospice Care and CALM.

We first became aware of Mark when he agreed to donate an amount of money to charity, matching the winning goal time and shirt number of the player scoring it in the derby against Watford during the behind-closed-doors matches of 2020-21.

The scorer at Kenilworth Road that afternoon, James Collins, and Harry Cornick got involved and Mark told them of his plan to cycle to every away match the follow season when they visited him to present him with a signed shirt on his doorstep soon after that famous victory.

Mark's story inspired us all, and I can honestly say that last season we all used to look forward to seeing his cheery face when we got off the coach at away grounds because we all knew what he'd put himself through to get there to watch his team.

He'd survived Storm Arwen and being blown off his bike on his way up to Blackpool, cycled to Swansea over three days, and even went to Hull on his own the week after we'd played there because he'd had to miss out on the matchday because of Covid!

What Mark did last season went above and beyond and he was a key factor in our success. Like all our fans, he's a part of our team and we were so happy for him when he was nominated for EFL Supporter of the Season.

It was a pleasure to have him with us at the EFL awards night, we were only sorry that he didn't bring home the silverware he deserved. He looked a million dollars cycling to Fulham in his dinner jacket and bow tie to win his bet with Gary Sweet, though!

Well done. Mark, you're a legend and everyone at Luton Town Football Club is so proud of what you achieved during a season to remember.

Come on you Hatters!

MICK HARFORD

# INTRODUCTION

So, if you have already made the commitment to purchase my book, firstly thank you. It should become obvious after a few chapters that writing a book does not come naturally to me, so hopefully you will persevere, and enjoy reading about my journey.

So why did I write a book and more importantly, why would I think anyone would be interested in reading about my year? Maybe out of loyalty to anyone that has crossed paths with me in the past or recently on my journey in the last year, or just a love for all things connected with Luton Town FC.

Anyway, the idea of sharing my experiences started as just a personal journal of my season-long adventures of following the mighty Hatters by the unconventional transport method of cycling on 2 wheels (obviously!) to raise awareness and donations for 3 fantastic charities.

The experience has put it all into perspective – having previously travelled by supporters' coach, car or train, I am sure when I revert back to a normal mode of transport, I will be more tolerant of the challenges faced. Another reflection on the year is to appreciate how lucky I have been to stay healthy in the current climate and to be able to fulfil my interests that I am so passionate about – that gives me incredible highs and lows, all part of the rollercoaster journey!

When I think of the life-changing difficulties that people face on a daily basis, especially through people I have touched as a result of the charities I have supported, it definitely puts everything into perspective and I am appreciative of everything we have.

I resisted the notion of writing a book of my experiences for a long time based on my thoughts that it wouldn't be that interesting writing about a bloke cycling to football games for a season. However, what I massively underestimated were the incredible people I have been fortunate to cross paths with on my challenge and the incredible memories created that will stay with me for the rest of my life. This was an aspect of the challenge that has been an unexpected bonus and has given me great pleasure. Thank you to everyone that has made the challenge such an incredible experience and I wanted the opportunity to share these memories with you all.

In addition, I wanted to share with you a small part of my background, for those that don't know me that well and more importantly, share some of my struggles, in the hope that if this helps just one person who can relate to my experiences, it will have all been worthwhile. So, I really hope that you gain some enjoyment from reading about my journey and experiences during the last season.

## 40 years of ups and downs following the Hatters

It is strange how things turn out and the direction life takes you. I moved school aged 14, made friends, was encouraged to attend a football game between Luton Town and Oldham on 25th April 1981 and the rest, as they say, is history – 40 years of ups and downs but memories that will stay with me forever.

My friendships formed through the love of football are too many to mention, but one, notably Mr John Dyer a previous work colleague, we developed a common interest in football, is a passionate QPR Supporter, and has been my best friend for nearly 40 years despite our allegiances to our respective clubs.

Anyway, back to my beloved Luton Town. It's impossible to cram 40 years of memories into one chapter but a few springs to mind.

My first full season was in 1981/82, watching us win League 1 while convincingly playing an exciting brand of football. My naive enthusiasm naturally presumed we would dominate world football in years to come. I would soon find out what a rollercoaster being a football supporter was.

The first season in the Championship (now called the Premiership) would end with us surviving relegation on the final game of the 82\83 season at Maine Road and celebrating the weekend in Blackpool as a 17-year-old.

When we were becoming an established Championship team, these were great days to be a Hatters fan, with great Cup runs, but I will never forget the heartbreak of the 1985 FA Cup semi-final defeat to Everton, the greatest injustice of a game and I felt absolutely devastated, was in tears for days and the most gutted I have ever been after a defeat.

It was the most incredible day seeing us beat Arsenal in the 1988 league cup final to win our first major trophy.

We reached the final in the following season. Losing to Nottingham Forest 3-1and struggled with our league form trying to avoid relegation, and a memorable date that springs to mind is 5$^{th}$ May 1990, where we had to beat Derby County and have other results go our way to stay up which we did due to a dramatic 3-2 win and to my surprise I was sent a photo from this game with me in the crowd. How different I look as a 24 year old, no signs of the grey hairs yet!

Unfortunately, relegation was unavoidable in the following 1991/92 season, which was the last season before the introduction of the premier league and the riches that brought.

It was heart-breaking to see the club on the brink of going out of business and having the injustice of the 30-points deduction and relegation out of the league in 2008/09, but we showed true spirit, winning the football league trophy the same year.

The non-league days until our promotion in 2013/14 were tough times but the character and togetherness shown is what makes us so strong today; no one would choose the non league years but the away trips we had to places like Nuneaton Borough, Dartford, Halifax, to name a few were part of our history and usually we outnumbered the home fans, our home games were a cup final for opposing teams not used to playing in front of 6,000 plus fans. The unshakeable bond the supporters have with the club and a special appreciation of the 2020 owners and Gary Sweet for saving our club, for always making decisions that have the best interests of the club and community at heart and for giving us a promising future to be excited about. I look at the present climate in football and the way clubs are run with disregard for the true values of the clubs and supporters and they are prepared to risk bankruptcy to chase the golden ticket. We are so grateful for what we have, thank you!

The last 7 years, seeing 3 promotions getting back to where we belong, have been an incredible journey of seeing the team evolve, with Nathan Jones playing a massive part at this stage, apart from the Stoke episode, which to be honest I was angry about beyond words and didn't want him back, but apologies accepted, bridges built, and we all moved forward. At the time of writing Nathan has left to join Southampton, but as a club, we grow stronger and move forward together.

Who can ever forget securing League 2 promotion away to Carlisle in 2018, one of my favourite away games? The train home was very lively from what I can remember!

Also, away at Notts County in 2019, celebrating promotion back to the championship.

It is said that the only loyalty shown to football clubs is by fans and that is true but as fans all we ask is for the team to show desire, passion, 100% commitment and pride to wear the shirt, and although players come and go, over the 40 years there have been many players who have held a special place in my heart and are responsible for some incredible experiences .

I couldn't possibly name them all, but to name a few: – Ricky Hill, Mal Donaghy, Brian Stein, Steve Foster,and David Pleat and David Preece, who are all legends. These were players from my earliest memories but more recently so many more players have made us proud and contributed to the success of the club – Kevin Nicholls,

Steve Howard, Marvin Johnson, James Justin, Curtis Davies, James Collins – I couldn't possibly name them all.

Sadly, some legends are no longer with us, like David Preece, Les Sealey and Ray Harford but left a lasting impression on the club.

The players that wear the shirt and grace Kenilworth road, are heroes to us, they are living out our dreams, and the current squad is no exception, through my challenge, I have been lucky enough to have had many conversations with a number of players and they all give their time and are friendly, respectful and approachable, now, I am the type of person that gets start struck easily, so to receive compliments from the players for my achievements is unreal, partly due to my low self-esteem, but I realise they are normal people like us all but lucky to play for this great club.

While players come and go and leave us with unforgettable memories, there is one man, that has done more for this club and has a special place in all our hearts and that is Luton legend Mick Harford. For most players, they are measured by their achievements on the pitch, Mick's loyalty to the club and community goes much further, Mick has been a hero of mine since 1984 when he first signed for the club, not only for his achievements on the pitch, but as manager through the difficult times, more recently, guiding us into the championship, and selfless in everything he has done for the club, I speak for everyone, that Mick holds a special place in all our hearts, so when it was known about his battles with Prostate Cancer, it was heart breaking news and everyone wanted to support him in beating it, despite the challenges faced, Mick is selfless in his support of the club and community, and I was only to pleased to help in any small way, raising awareness and donations through my challenge. Mick is such an inspirational, genuine, decent and humble bloke and it has been an absolute pleasure and an honour to have had the opportunity to get to know him during the last year.

I find it difficult to put into words what this club means to me. Over 40 years I feel I have been on a journey with Luton Town through the ups and downs – personally, as well as the ups and downs the club have experienced. The friendships made, the memories that last a lifetime through the highs and lows and the importance that the club places on supporters and the community give me a special feeling of pride and optimism that I hope will continue for many years to come as we move to Power Court and a new, exciting future. Thank you. Come on you Hatters.

# My struggles with my mental health

A big part of me that has influenced my journey of ups and downs throughout my life has been my struggle with my mental health and I felt it was an important subject to share, however difficult it may be to relive it. My hope is that by sharing my experiences, it may help one person to realise that there is help available and everyone deserves to be happy.

So back in my teenage years I was bullied at school and as a result was introverted – to this day I'm not sure what impact this has had on me. In my later teenage years I was quite reserved, withdrawn and didn't mix well. Now, back in the eighties depression wasn't recognised as an illness, if you were depressed you were told to 'get on with it' 'stop feeling sorry for yourself' – these were normal responses. I didn't know I was depressed, I just thought I was being miserable although my thoughts were much deeper, and I didn't think I had a future to look forward to. I began to put on weight, my self-esteem and confidence were low, and my only escapes were football and running, which I got into initially for a few months to lose weight, but which lasted nearly 10 years and helped with my self-esteem until wear and tear on my knees meant I had to stop.

Moving forward, there were several periods in my life where I struggled that I want to share. In 2004, when I was 38, I remember going through a really difficult time. One constant throughout my struggles is my best friend John of 40 years who has always been there for me as I have been for him. So, it was around the time that my mum passed away, leading to feelings of guilt, low self-worth and periods of depression. It was at this time I had deep thoughts about suicide, not deserving to be happy, and irrational thoughts that I wouldn't be missed. This time, I sought the help of a counsellor. Now this was around the time I was due to go to South Africa on my own to watch cricket but at the time it was hard enough to leave the house. Speaking to someone who didn't know me, didn't judge me and just listened was a great help, there were even aspects of my life that I didn't realise had an impact on me until I discussed it with the counsellor, this helped me to focus on taking positive steps whilst understanding my thoughts were real and normal. Some of the steps were to write down a balance sheet trying to focus on achievements, however small. The counselling wasn't an overnight eureka moment and for periods it was hard to go over aspects of my past, but the counsellor helped me to understand and appreciate the journey I was taking and slowly I felt more positive about the future.

I appreciated that there would be bumps in the road on my journey but I was looking to head in the right direction.

*it is perfectly okay to admit you're not okay*

Fast-forward to 2018, and I was struggling again with depression. Now, I don't recall one specific moment that triggered the feelings but sometimes it is a build-up of struggling to cope rather than one significant event that triggers this. It was noticed I was withdrawn at work, not communicating and going home where I could be alone with my thoughts, not always a good thing. I would withdraw from any social events, all I wanted was to be alone. I could go to football and cycle without having to interact with anyone. I had family abroad so I could pretend everything was fine, but it wasn't. Once again, I had feelings that I didn't deserve to be happy, and everyone would be better off without me around. Feelings of being worthless and feelings of anxiety. Anyone who has felt the same will relate to feeling helpless and wanting the pain to go away, I contacted my doctor, who subscribed anti-depressants and recommended counselling. I avoided this, despite knowing how previous counselling had helped. All I could think was that I would be wasting their time and others were more deserving.

My employer, CarShop, work was very supportive and even more so when I had setbacks a few years later.

It is so important to have someone to talk to, even if it's just someone who will listen and won't judge. It really does help to know you don't have to struggle alone and suffer in silence and there is a way out, other people have had the same struggles, and everyone deserves to be happy. It would have been easy for people to see me as 'Mark is just in a bad mood' or tell me to snap out of it or cheer up, so if you have someone, friend or family member, who seems to be struggling, just asking them if they are ok is such a big thing for them – knowing they have someone they can talk to who will listen is massive. I know this from experience.

The anti-depressants were a big help, but I didn't want to be too reliant on them, and my cycling was my escape and throwing myself into charity rides helped me take the focus away from myself. My low self-esteem, self-worth and self-confidence have always been an issue for me, and I don't receive praise easily. I recognised that I didn't always want to feel like this, and I started to read self-help books. There is no right or wrong way to cope and it's different for everyone but asking for help is the first step to recovery and taking one day at a time.

I remember going to a work seminar which had a social evening function. I managed the day seminar and was able to interact, keeping in the background on a business level, but the anxiety of the evening function was too much for me, so I made my apologies and left before the evening. Despite this, I appreciated that I was making progress just to attend the day and that I was heading in the right direction.

It would take the COVID-19 pandemic in 2020 for me to have another significant setback, which I appreciate was the same for many people trying to cope. For myself, prior to COVID-19 I was going to football, working in an office environment, participating in cycle activities and suddenly all of this was taken away. I was working from home with no interaction with anyone, with the exception of my friend John, who was staying with me. I wouldn't see anyone or speak to anyone and once again I distanced myself from the outside world and being alone with my thoughts I started to spiral into a depressive state of mind. This went on for several weeks with irrational suicidal thoughts consuming me almost daily, finding it difficult to sleep, being short of breath and unable to function properly.

My employer, Carshop Work was extremely supportive, especially, my managers, Haston and Paula who recognised that I was struggling and suggested I went back into the office for a few days a week, which at first I agreed to. Although I had long periods in the office alone, there was some interaction and it helped to have a routine, but I was still having unhealthy thoughts consume my thinking. I always thought that having struggled before, I would recognise the signs and be able to act before it got a lot worse, but it was like I was on a rollercoaster and I couldn't get off, or another comparison was being in a dark room with no lights or doors with no way out. I was restless, couldn't sleep, short of breath and would have suicidal tendencies that felt like it was the only way out and if I ended my life the pain would go away forever.

Through conversations with my manager, Haston, Counselling was recommended to me through the companies works counselling support service. I wasn't sure at first, and knowing that speaking to a counsellor had been previously beneficial, I don't know why I resisted, but I'm so grateful that I was persuaded to speak to someone, like I mentioned before, it is so easy to give up on people, when all people in a similar position want is someone to listen and to know there is help available for them and so I started a programme of counselling along with increased medication of anti-depressants.

The counsellor was a great comfort to me, although it was difficult to talk about some subjects. She just listened and at the beginning of each session there was a range of questions that had set answers. The answers would range from' frequently' to 'not at all,' and these questions helped the counsellor to understand my state of mind from session to session. The counsellor would ask thought-provoking questions and, in some sessions, it was difficult to talk about my feelings and thoughts, but they made me think differently about my emotions and experiences. It was helpful when the counsellor gave me several exercises ranging from a gratitude diary to focussing on daily achievements, a balance sheet of where I was at, to a mood cycle based on how I reacted to events and circumstances. I related this to a cycle ride – as I said before it's different for everyone. It was helpful to write everything down and over the sessions I felt I was making progress. At this stage the dark, deep thoughts were becoming less frequent – another sign I was making progress.

During the period when I was spending time on my own, I spent time listening to various podcasts, and one in particular that I enjoyed was the 'Oh When The Town', hosted by Luke.G, Dave & Luke.B, I found it enjoyable listening to the discussions of all things Luton Town. At this stage, I was still finding it difficult to mix on a social level but joining in with the podcast and sharing my thoughts and opinions, helped me feel like we were all down the pub chatting about football, but still in my safety comfort zone of my 4 walls. Although they didn't realise it at the time, their podcast was a great help to me to the point of feeling more positive about life in a small way, so thank you!

I was to have another setback. A night out with friends had been arranged weeks in advance but during the week of the night out I started getting anxious to the point that it was consuming my thoughts with fear and dread and I was getting stressed. Negative, irrational thoughts were coming back, and I made my excuses and didn't go. I explained to the counsellor that it felt like I had taken a backward step.

The counsellor was good, and we talked about it at length. I would be on my own for Christmas, but I had coping mechanisms from the counsellor to help, and I was able to cope. It was a massive help just to have people to talk to. Prior to Christmas I had gone back to the office full-time; however, there was another lockdown in the new year.

I felt that I was in a better place to cope with this lockdown, and it was a case of taking small steps forward. This was 8 months ago, and I feel in a much better place now for several reasons. I look back to the dark place I was in and never want to go back there although I appreciate there will be bumps in the road along the way, but I couldn't have coped without the support of the counselling, friends and work colleagues, also the away cycle challenge has given me the opportunity to focus on others and not myself, whilst keeping me busy.

I appreciate that everyone has their own struggles and copes in their own way but by sharing mine, I really hope that I give hope to even just one person to reach out for help if you're struggling and that it does get better day by day and there are people to help, and everyone deserves to be happy. One of my favourite sayings is: 'It's ok not to be ok'.

At this point, as part of my self-improvement, I wanted to take the focus away from myself and focus on being able to make a small difference to others less fortunate than myself and this was where I came up with the idea of another charity cycle challenge. It was a big step outside of my comfort zone – the actual physical training, I knew I could prepare for, but the social interaction required to promote an event would be less comfortable. But I had set my mind on doing something combining my passions of cycling and football and as the plans started to be put into place, it really did help to have a focus and helped with my struggles.

## Season 2020/2021 – COVID-19 and Watford rivalry resumed

We started the season in COVID-19 lockdown. I wouldn't have believed that I would go a whole season without seeing my beloved Luton Town live, and not being able to be part of the few thousand able to attend a few of the games, so the season was spent watching on ifollow. During this time I was really struggling with my mental health, which I covered in the last chapter, and was not able to attend games and see anyone, with my exposure being limited to solo cycles and working from home.

Anyway, back to the season ahead – of course the fixtures being released would only mean every Hatters fan had eyes for just 2 fixtures against our bitter rivals, Watford, relegated from the premiership. My dislike for Watford goes back to the 81/82 season but due to our decline down the leagues it meant locking horns had been put on hold, for 14 years to be exact. I will come back to those 2 games later but summing up the season it was a positive season on the pitch, with stability in the Championship and being able to achieve a top half finish with some significant notable results. The team was evolving as we established ourselves in the championship after our dramatic escape from relegation in the 2019/20 season with Nathan Jones playing a significant part! The signing of Adebayo from Walsall in January, the loan-signing of Dewsbury-Hall from Leicester and Jordan Clark to name a few, strengthened the team positively and whilst perceived bigger teams like Sheffield Wednesday and Derby County were fighting relegation, we were in the unusual position of mid-table security. In recent years this has been rare as we climbed the leagues from the conference and stabilised in the championship. To reflect that in 6 short years we have climbed from the dark days of the Conference to the Championship is nothing short of staggering and has been an incredible journey and I'm excited about the journey in coming seasons. A massive part of the rise has been due to the 2020 board and Gary Sweet for stabilising the club along with the supporters fighting for the future of the club after it almost went to the wall. I look at other clubs that are suffering the same struggles and I am grateful to have a club and owners that care for the supporters, the community and the future of the club.

Anyway, back to the Watford fixtures. Having waited for 14 years, although I couldn't go, the anticipation had been building ever since the fixtures came out. I realised how much I had missed these games but the game at Vicarage Road would end in massive disappointment with a 1-0 defeat, despite knowing how much it meant to the fans. It was a lacklustre performance with the turning point being James Collins missing from a few yards out and struggling to create anything significant.

So, we had to wait for 7 months for the returning fixture, which happened on a sunny April day. We simply had to win this game, as we had waited 14 years and Watford were on the brink of getting promoted back to the premiership and we couldn't let them have bragging rights. The players were under no illusions how big this game was for the club.

Such was my desperation to see us win the game that I made a pledge on Twitter to make a donation to charity (Keech Hospice and Mind charity because of my struggles with mental health) if we won to the value of the minute of the winning goal plus the shirt number of the player who scored it. I didn't really give it much thought as the day unfolded. I arrived at Nick's for the game on a tense afternoon in the sunshine, nervous, but optimistic that we would deliver. Come on you Hatters!

We were at it from the first minute and it became obvious that we wanted it more, the pressing movement passing the desire, but we still got to half time 0-0. The second half largely followed the same pattern, then the dramatic and significant moment in the 78th minute. Adebayo beat Foster to the ball inside the area and was crudely taken out by the referee, who had no hesitation in pointing to the spot penalty. Yes! Come on, Luton, this is the moment, but hold on – if Adebayo was unable to continue from the challenge, who was going to take the penalty? The substitution was made, and James Collins came on and, incredibly, his first touch would be to take the penalty. Now, as everyone who knows me knows, James Collins is a hero of mine and to score the winning goal would make him a Luton legend.

Everyone held their breath, no need to panic, as he coolly slotted it into the corner, sending Foster the wrong way. 1-0 and– there were celebrations everywhere and just 12 minutes to hold on. A very long 12 minutes before the referee blew his whistle. We had beaten them at last – the bragging rights, the celebrations – I was buzzing with uncontrollable excitement, an amazing feeling! Boys, you did us proud. I love this club.

So, in the aftermath of the celebration, it dawned on me that my pledge – it had been a 78$^{th}$-minute winning goal and James Collins had shirt number 19 – equalled a donation of £97.

At the time I thought it was a nice little donation for the charities, after sharing my commitment to fulfil my promise on social media, and I thought that would be it. Well, how wrong I was. The euphoria of beating Watford led to the wider Luton community coming together to support great charities, resulting in a staggering £1,000 plus raised in 3 days, including a donation from James Collins and his partner, who both had an affiliation with Keech Hospice Care and also a number of donations from the club. The irony wasn't lost on me that I raised just over £1,400 sat on my backside cheering the Hatters when cycling from Land's End to John O' Groats had raised less.

The club really do care about the fans and the community. Stu Hammond had been a huge support promoting this and once again I thought that was that, and once again I was wrong. I got a message asking if I was home and thought nothing of it, then to my shock and surprise I opened the door the next day to Stu and Harry Cornick, bringing me a signed shirt. Shocked was an understatement, it was an incredible experience. Harry was happy to chat for what seemed like ages and was a genuinely decent guy, happy to give up his time. I'm not sure if the players truly appreciate what it means to fans for them to give up their time even for just a few minutes – it might seem a small gesture to them, but my experience meant so much to me and I will be forever grateful. There were plenty more examples of this for me in later chapters, so shock number 2 was a surprise FaceTime chat with a hero of mine, James Collins, a day I will never forget. Just a few days later Collo left for Cardiff, and my friends did ask me what I'd said to him to make him leave! My Luton heroes play a big part in my life, but the team evolves, and new heroes are born. Thanks, Collo, for 4 incredible years. I loved your desire, work rate, commitment, team spirit and bucketloads of goals during our rise to the Championship.

# My Mad Hatter Away Cycle Challenge

Back in April 2020 it was my intention to cycle to the last away game at Hull to raise funds for Keech Hospice in memory of young Ethan, who was a young boy and Luton fan battling with Cancer who was cared for by Keech Hospice, who had sadly passed away. Unfortunately, COVID-19 took over the world and football with fans was cancelled. Since then, it was always at the back of my mind, asking myself if this challenge would be possible over a season, although I dismissed the idea due to logistics – would winter cycling, be supported? The thought wouldn't leave me. I would look at fixtures and think, what if?! Then the incredible response and generosity from the Collo /Watford goal donations created some momentum and got me known a bit more within the club and on social media. Then I started looking at the logistical planning. So then I was telling Stu and Harry Cornick I was going to do it for charity. No going back now, eeeek! The usual thoughts from sensible, logical friends were, 'You're going to do what?' ;'You're crazy' and 'Why don't you do just a few games?' My mind was made up, no going back, or to use a phrase: 'The train has left the station and it isn't backing up.' One of my driving forces was to raise awareness and funds for charities I am passionate about. I've touched on my struggles with mental health and had benefitted from counselling and support and wanted to give back and reach out to let people know there is help available. In addition, I had learned more about prostate cancer through my dad and Luton legend Mick Harford and wanted to share the message on my rides. Finally, I am passionate about the work that Keech Hospice do for children and adults with life-limiting illnesses and also wanted to support them.

So, ahead of the new season, the first hurdle had been crossed as the Bobbers Travel Club agreed to help me get me and my bike home after every away game. Without their help, this challenge wouldn't have been possible – not even me and my crazy challenges could get to and from away games.

I waited nervously for the fixtures to be released. Would they be kind to me with trips to Middlesbrough, Swansea, Blackpool, and Preston, to name a few? A few winners and losers came out, home on Boxing Day, short distances in winter months of January and February but finishing on a London ride and Swansea and Blackpool in December and Middlesbrough in March. Like my beloved Luton Town, I don't do things easily. I love a challenge and I got one.

So, the fixtures were released, followed by months of planning, hours online searching cycling apps, accommodation options, agreeing to take leave from my employers over the season and a summer of training to prepare myself for the challenge ahead, although nothing really prepares you for the winter months. The navigation and mechanical issues for someone with a poor sense of direction really are a challenge but every challenge I take on, I put everything into it. There is a saying: 'If you fail to prepare you are preparing to fail' and I was determined to make this challenge a success.

From the football perspective, it had been a busy summer, with 8 new exciting signings, to strengthen squad whilst saying goodbye to some favourites who had served us well during our rise to the championship. Also, the squad was evolving to ensure we kept improving on our satisfying 12th place from last season. Personally, I was happy to forfeit my discount on my season ticket, I just wanted to give back to the club who were so important to me and wanted to help in difficult times, and I knew the money would be spent wisely. We are so lucky to have owners that have the best interest of the club and fans at heart.

So, the summer brought several pre-season fixtures. The first one I attended was Bedford away, a chance to see new players. At the end of the game Harry Cornick had seen me and was interested to know about my challenge – a small gesture but so nice and appreciative and one I wasn't expecting. I was even surprised he remembered me, although that was as much to do with my low self-esteem as anything.

So, ahead of the season's away challenge I decided to gauge the challenge by cycling to Borehamwood and back in the absence of away coaches. The weather was seriously hot and the journey there was 45 miles getting lost around Hemel Hempstead and St Albans but I arrived in time. It was a nice day catching up with everyone, enjoying the sunshine, seeing a 2-1 win and a stunning winner from Carlos Mendez Gomez (a great signing with potential). Borehamwood was the first away fan outing so I set off home, fatigued by the journey there and sitting in the sun. I took the shorter route home, not one of my better decisions cycling on the busy A414 to Hemel Hempstead (those that know it, it is the busy dual carriageway alongside the M1). 10 miles from home I got a puncture in Leighton Buzzard. A generous guy offered to help as he lived around the corner, and he asked me about my ride. When I told him, he sponsored me, and I was up and running with my first donation, a bonus of having a puncture. It had been an eventful day but an insight into the season's challenge ahead.

So, I just wanted to share my experiences of the away challenges, both from a cycling and a football perspective and also some of the incredible people I have met. Although most of the people I met go to the games, a lot of them I wouldn't have crossed paths with them prior to my challenge, and I feel richer for knowing you all and sharing conversations and I have been blown away by your encouraging comments. I signed up for cycling, football and raising funds and awareness for the charities but there have been so many more experiences that have touched me that I will share with you on the journey in future chapters.

The first official away game of the season was Stevenage in the carabao cup. Come on you Hatters! Prior to this game, I was receiving positive feedback about the challenge and had already received £341 in donations, which put me in good spirits ahead of the first challenge.

## Tuesday 10th August 2021 at 7.45pm - Stevenage Borough

So, my Away Cycle Challenge started with a gentle introduction and a nice short cycle to Stevenage Borough, which was going to be 30.5 miles. Even though this wouldn't be a demanding ride it was the start of my challenge and I wanted to get off to a good start with no dramas. The bike was all checked the night before and I worked in the morning and left home about 3.30 pm. I was lucky to have a nice sunny day to start my challenge. I was going to make the most of the weather, enjoying what was a rare occurrence during the summer.

The route took me a familiar route through Woburn, Husborne Crawley and out to Eaton Bray where I had a halfway stop at 15 miles for a catch-up with a friend, James, before my onward route which took me through Hitchin. The navigation app couldn't decide how to get out of Hitchin so reverted to a direct route to Stevenage using the google map (you will notice this is a common theme during the season!) This was about 6-ish so I was starting to hit traffic. The route took me over the A1M roundabout along a dual carriageway into Stevenage. Another common theme as I get near to the ground is the familiar access roads from when I had driven to the grounds on previous visits as I leave the less familiar cycle routes.

So, I arrived at the ground about 6.30. In total the cycle was 30.5 miles, and the cycling time was 1 hour and 51 minutes. With just 1,371 feet elevation and 743 calories burned, it wasn't too demanding. I had completed my first challenge and took what would be a mandatory photo outside the Stevenage FC sign with my bike, courtesy of accommodating police officers.

The team coach arrived, and I managed to catch a few words with Harry Cornick. The standard procedure on arrival at the grounds is to contact Les/Stewart from the Bobbers Travel Club, who had generously agreed to transport me and the bike home after each away game, which was such a brilliant gesture, as without their help this challenge wouldn't have been possible. Anyway, there was some confusion where the coach would be parking but after several messages from Les I found the coach and was met by some friendly faces and was able to leave the bike on the coach.

I made the short walk to the ground and queued to enter. Because of the warm weather, I stayed in my Lycra cycling shorts with my Luton shirt. My first observation was to keep my cycling jersey on so I had some pockets. Hope I didn't smell, might not have anyone sat next to me!

Now, it was the first game with supporters attending so the checks going into the ground were very much like airport checks although they took one look at me and decided I wasn't hiding anything, as lycra cycling shorts aren't the normal clothing choice for going to football so I did get a few comments. One was a jokey smiling, 'So you cycled here?' When I said, 'Yes, I'm cycling to all away games,' I'm not sure if he at first believed me. I got several positive, encouraging comments and people wanting to know about the challenge. This shocked me and would be a regular theme at all of the away games. When I had been planning the challenge, I really wasn't expecting much response. I was just a bloke on a bike following my team, trying to raise a few pounds for charity. Maybe this is partly due to my low self-esteem, self-confidence and self-worth.

Regarding the game, Luton Town had started the league campaign with a convincing 3-0 win at home to Peterborough, an emotional return to Kenilworth Road after COVID-19. So, this Cup game, whilst wanting to win, I felt was about giving some players some minutes and we got to see some new players. Admiral Muskwe looked impressive and caught the eye, also Sam Beckwith was making his senior debut. Having said that, Stevenage were up for the game and set the pace, taking the lead after 2 minutes. They took the lead twice but probably against the run of play we went into halftime at 2-2, confident that our class would show and run out comfortable winners. The second half was a stalemate with half chances for both sides not taken so the game went straight to penalties. To be honest, we had a shocker, missing all 3 penalties and losing 3-0. I can't remember a team losing a penalty shoot-out without converting at least one penalty but despite the defeat it was great to be back at an away game and it gave some of the players some much needed game time.

So, it was back on the coach to make the journey home. My route home after away games in the south is to take the coach back to Flitwick and cycle the final 11 to 12 miles home. So, on this occasion

I got off the coach at 11.20pm and started my 12-mile cycle home that took me 47 minutes with 547 feet elevation on a familiar route through Steppingley, Aspley Guise and Woburn Sands so I got home just after 12.15am and as I reflected on the evening and my first challenge completed it would be gone 1am before I considered catching up on sleep. Come on you Hatters!

The days after the Stevenage game were a period of brief reflection whilst planning ahead for the West Brom game. The messages and donations were so satisfying – for the short period either side of the Stevenage game, £335 had been donated, bringing the total to £676, beyond my expectations for the first week of the season.

# Saturday 14th August at 3 pm - West Bromwich Albion

I had a short turnaround from Stevenage (which would be a regular occurrence) until Away Cycle Challenge 2 to West Bromwich Albion. . For reasons unknown, EFL have decided to have back-to-back away games followed by back-to-back home games – it seems gone are the days of alternating between home/away games.

So, my northern cycle challenges usually set off from Newport Pagnell, where I leave my car at my friend's parents' house. For this challenge would be an early start at 6.25 am.. The northern rides head off through Stoke Goldington towards Northampton. It would take a few of these rides before I got used to navigating around the outskirts of Northampton via Duston, so I followed the Komoot cycling app towards Kenilworth through to Solihull. It was largely uneventful although on one occasion the navigation app took me down what I thought was a country lane, only to be stopped and asked if I was lost by the owner whose drive I was cycling down. We both saw the funny side. I always knew it would be an adventure!

I arrived on the outskirts of Solihull, having made good progress at approximately 50 miles. Now the app said about 25 miles to go – plenty of time to spare, even arriving at the ground early, or so I thought. How difficult could the last third of the journey be? Well, it involved cycling through Birmingham city traffic on a Saturday lunchtime – to say it was interesting was an understatement. Anyway, en route to the Hawthorns, not far to go or so I thought, the navigation told me I'd arrived but I couldn't see the stadium. I stopped and asked directions and the response I got was, 'Which stadium are you looking for?' I then knew I wasn't that close, I was in Oldbury, and it had started to rain.

Eventually, I was back on the right track to the Hawthorns in the rain. I knew I wasn't far away but still couldn't see the stadium. I cycled round an industrial estate a few times, taking directions from a comedian sending me in the wrong direction, and eventually I saw a few Baggies supporters in shirts so I followed then down a cycle path along a railway track path and through an estate which brought me out where I could see the ground. I had finally arrived at the Hawthorns, which had taken me 86 miles, 5 hours 43 minutes of cycling time, 3,826 feet elevation and 1,926 calories burned – but I had finally completed Away Cycle Challenge 2.

In the days leading up to the West Brom game, I had contacted them asking if they could share my challenge on social media, not really having any expectations that they would. To my surprise they kindly agreed, and the challenge received positive feedback again. The impact of this became apparent as I waited outside the ground waiting to hear from Les about the arrival of the Bobbers Travel coach, minding my own business with my bike. I was taken aback by the good wishes from both Luton and West Brom supporters – the power of social media and the wider footballing community coming together for the fantastic charities became evident and would be a regular theme in months to come. In the following days , seeing donations from Baggies fans was brilliant.

By this point, the rain was getting heavier, and the coach arrived about 2.20 pm, so I was able to get into the ground ahead of kick-off. I took my seat in hope rather than expectation. West Brom were one of the favourites for promotion and this would be a tough game, which was the case as they dominated early proceedings and led 2-0 by half-time, with an unfortunate own goal from Kal Naismith. We hadn't settled into the game, and it took a twist with a sickening injury to Jordan Clark just after the hour after a collision with their keeper. If that challenge had happened anywhere else it would have been a free kick and possibly a sending off, and to make it worse we then went 3-0 behind and it seemed like a heavy defeat was likely but to their credit they never gave up, Nathan changed the formation, we were more aggressive, moving the ball forward quicker and Harry Cornick pulled a goal back with 20 minutes to go. There was a swing in momentum encouraged with 17 minutes of injury-time shown due to Jordan Clark's injury, and roared on by the fantastic Hatters' support, Pelly then scored after 98 minutes but West Brom managed to hang on. Everyone was of the opinion another 5 minutes, and we would have got a point but a poor first hour had cost us. Anyway, back on the coach and back home after a long day, to find another £205 had been donated over the weekend. Fantastic support for the team and my challenge. Come on you Hatters!

## Tuesday 17th August at 7.45pm - Barnsley

The Barnsley challenge would see the culmination of a hectic 7 days with the first 3 away games during that period, trying to recover between challenges but also making sure that I was ticking over with steady high-cadence leg spin sessions. I had learnt to listen to my body, gauging my energy levels using the data I had available. With Barnsley being a midweek game and the weather forecast looking promising, I decided to cycle there in one day. I felt good ahead of a long day where I was due to cycle more than 130 miles even though I felt nervous. If I was to arrive on time, it required the navigation plan to run smoothly, while taking on board enough carbs and protein to keep energy levels high.

The Barnsley game was going to be the longest distance covered in one day on the challenge and as with West Brom, I asked for support from Barnsley to promote my ride as well as from Luton Town and the response and encouragement was amazing, adding extra pressure to that I had imposed on myself. The cycling is hard enough without extra pressure, why do I do this to myself? Although from my planning it appeared I would arrive in plenty of time, I had to navigate busy cities such as Northampton, Leicester, Nottingham ring roads and Rotherham en route to Barnsley so breaking down the day into intervals was key to my planning. Another early start was required so I was on the road by 6.18 am.

The beginning of the route took a familiar path heading out towards Northampton, on the busy A45 for one junction then through Northampton and out on the A5199 towards Leicester. This was a long, straight road through a few villages, and although a boring route, it was nice to switch off the brain from focusing on the navigation and bashing out the miles, counting in 5/10-mile intervals or elevation landmarks. With endurance cycling, you have a lot of thinking time, it can be a very lonely alone with your thoughts but also nice depending on your state of mind. Anyway, I arrived at Wigston just outside Leicester. At 45 miles, it was just under 3 hours so a good point to stop at a Costa. I checked my phone and was shocked at the number of messages on Twitter and also the donations were coming in. It is extremely rewarding and satisfying knowing that what I am doing is helping the charities in a small way. I'm not sure if everyone who leaves messages realises how much of a lift it gives me, it means so much.

The route was going to get more complicated, so it was time to engage the brain again, trying to avoid busy roads as I headed out towards Nottingham. I ended up on a busy dual carriageway for what seemed like ages but just before Loughborough I turned off and back onto the quieter roads. I was ticking off the miles: 60, 65, 70 miles achieved towards Nottingham. I knew I was passing the halfway mark. I always remember a saying : 'The good news is you're halfway, the bad news is you're half way.' It means that it depends on how the body is holding up and how mentally strong you feel. On the really long rides I play a game of miles done versus miles to go. I also treat 90 miles like a football game, anything to get me through.

Anyway I approached Nottingham and I had the option of busy built-up traffic or ring road traffic. I took the latter, and it was now 1 pm and I hit the lunchtime traffic, which was a bit scary! I survived and headed towards Sutton-in-Ashfield near Mansfield; en route to Bolsover, but I was really struggling physically. I'm guilty of not taking in enough fluid as was the case here and I found a pub at the 90-mile point. It was about 3 pm and I'd been about 8/9 hours on the road and I still had another 40 miles to go and needed a pick-me-up.

An hour's rest, recovery, food and checking on the messages of encouragement was the pick-me-up I needed. I gave the legs a pep talk and I set off again. The weather had been kind to me with dry, sunny intervals but not too warm and mild winds. Now as I left Nottinghamshire behind and headed into Yorkshire towards Rotherham, I noticed the elevation becoming more challenging. I crossed off 100 miles – just 6 sets of 5 miles and I would have arrived. I reached Rotherham and I knew I was close and needed a final push. Crossing off the checkpoints with the last few climbs into Barnsley, I finally arrived about 6.15 pm, 12 hours after setting off – 133 miles cycled with 8-and-a-half hours actual cycling time with a challenging 5,141 feet elevation, burning 3,100 calories. I had finally completed Away Cycle Challenge 3.

The first friendly face I met was John Pyper, and I posed for photos outside the Barnsley sign. Barnsley had been incredibly encouraging and really supported my challenge. It helps so much when they back it and share it on social media, so I met a few people to say thank you before finding the coach to offload my bike and speak to well-wishers and get ready for the game and take my seat, where I received more encouraging support.

Regarding the game, Nathan had made 5 changes from the West Brom game, with Admiral Muskwe, Tom Lockyer, Cameron Jerome and Henri Lansbury all starting. We made the perfect start with Amari'i Bell finishing from an Elijah Adabayo cross. On reflection, it was a solid, disciplined performance. Barnsley had the majority of possession but only created a few chances and Simon Sluga was assured to keep a clean sheet as we held on for a deserved win. It is always satisfying to travel away and see an away win, even more so when I had had a long cycle to get there. I was sat next to a guy called

Mike and we chatted about the game and my challenge and Mike would be a big supporter of my challenge over the season, one of many friendships that I would make .

The coach ride home was a long journey too, with traffic accidents causing delays, so we didn't get back to Newport Pagnell services until about 1 am. I was busy unloading the bike from the coach and when I turned around, to my amazement Harry Cornick was standing there waiting to chat after the team coach arrived at the same time. Stood chatting to Harry in a service station car park at 1 am was something totally unexpected and a surprise. I was so pleased and excited, and it completed a brilliant day. Time to get home and catch up on sleep.

# Mainstream media interest

When I set out on my challenge, I wasn't sure that a bloke cycling to football games would create much interest and I certainly am not the type that craves attention. I am a guy that avoids attention largely due to my low self-confidence and self-worth, but I was prepared to step outside my comfort zone for the benefit of the charities if the situation arose.

The first occasion I was unprepared for was a message from Three Counties Radio wanting me to go on Justin Dealey's programme to talk about my event on 11th August, the day after the Stevenage game. This, I believe, had a positive impact on donations and I was made to feel relaxed so overcame my nerves.

The next period of attention in my event was following the Barnsley game. On my ride to Barnsley, I received a message from Anglia TV wanting to do an interview for their news programme and this was arranged for 20th August but before this happened, I was asked to do another Three Counties Radio interview on 19th August with Justin. Again, I was made to feel relaxed. I was feeling less relaxed about the Anglia TV recording. They were also interviewing Sarah from Keech Hospice and it was a pleasure to finally meet her after exchanging messages about my support for the hospice. Everyone connected to Keech is so inspirational and I'm always happy to support the work they do.

So, as for the Anglia TV recording, it started with some action shots which lasted about an hour and helped to take my mind off the interview. I was still feeling sick with nerves. I tried to stay calm and answer the questions and be enthusiastic. The interviewer was really nice and must be used to interviewing all types of people from all walks of life. The interview went well until the questions focused on my struggles with depression and it all came back to me and I got emotional and tearful, but they were good, I regained composure and finished the filming.

Such was my perception of myself I couldn't watch the programme, never mind wait to receive feedback. It was like a hiding behind the sofa with hands over my eyes moment but there was no need to worry as it turned out well.

The impact of the coverage of both TV and radio along with social media posts from Luton Town and everyone else was staggering. The week of the Barnsley game and the coverage had resulted in donations of £1,150 taking the total raised to nearly £1,900 – considering this was just from 3 away games I was blown away by the response. I was thrilled for the charities that they were benefitting from the exposure and generosity of everyone.

Further exposure was arranged after a zoom chat with Dan from the media team at Luton Town, who published an article in the programme for the Sheffield United game. The article was personal and detailed my struggles with depression. I felt it was important to reach out to people who had their own struggles and needed help – if, by my exposure, I had helped one person, it would be worth it all The football club had been and continues to be so supportive of my challenge and the charities – the club really does care about the supporters and the community.

## Saturday 11th September at 3 pm - Blackburn Rovers

Blackburn was the first game back after an international break, so I had time to recover from the Barnsley ride and to fit in some training miles including a 70-mile endurance ride and a club ride. These rides were important to maintain fitness levels without over-training. It's always difficult to get the balance right with a mixture of experience and listening to my body.

Although I was rested it was another period of back-to-back away challenges with both Blackburn and Bristol City within 5 days. Blackburn was the first away challenge that would be split over 2 days with a significant section of the ride on the day before. I had estimated that it would be a total distance of 160 miles with 120 miles on the Friday. I had planned the route and pre-booked accommodation in Macclesfield though Airbnb to keep the cost down, with the added bonus that I would have the house to myself. The challenge with this arrangement was that there was no flexibility, as I had to get to Macclesfield by the end of the day.

The Blackburn ride was another early start, and I was up around 4.30 am after about 4 hours' sleep – it's always a restless night's sleep the night before a challenge. I was on the road for 6.08 am, a similar start on quiet roads with a few wrong turns trying to find Duston, but finally the penny dropped! The route took me to Lutterworth and I entered Leicestershire without further drama. This time of year it is always difficult to gauge choice of clothing still mild enough for shirts but thermal layers to keep the chill out. I had decided to take my first break at 50 miles around the 3 and a half hour mark by mid/late morning at a nice cafe for a 45-minute rest at a place called Stoney Stanton in Leicestershire.

The route took me through Burton-on-Trent and headed in the direction of Uttoxeter, reaching a place called Sudbury on the Derbyshire/Staffordshire border. I had reached this point at 90 miles and unfortunately a missed turning took me onto a busy dual carriageway, and I lost my sense of direction, spending 7 miles trying to get back on track. Up to now the elevation had been consistent without being spectacularly demanding, Having said that, fatigue had set in during the long day and I stopped for a rest at 100 miles, taking in millionaire shortbread and ice cream – not my chosen recovery nutrition but I needed treats!

I still had 30 miles to get to Macclesfield because of the detour. Now, I knew from the route-planning that the journey through Staffordshire covered the edge o the peaks. Already fatigued, the climbs were brutally hard, seemed to last for ages and drained what energy I had left. At certain stages of the climbs, it was an effort to keep the pedals turning, and it became a mental challenge as much as physical. I was feeling sick by the final climb, but fortunately the final 5 miles into Macclesfield were downhill and I finally arrived around 5 pm

127 miles were cycled in the day with 8 and a half hours' cycling time, and 7,600 feet elevation, burning over 3,000 calories. The evening was spent refuelling and recovering with a few well-earned ciders.

Saturday would be a less demanding day, starting at 8.40 am with just over 40 miles to Elwood Park. It would be a slow start to wake up the legs after the previous day's efforts but would involve navigating central Manchester traffic with a stop for breakfast at McDonald's at 9.30 am. It was a bit of a shock – now I know I'm getting old but either the dress code has changed, or I walked into a night club serving McDonald's. Oh, to be young again!

The final ride to Elwood Park was uneventful with a few climbs to finish and I arrived about 1 pm to complete away Cycle Challenge 4 with a total of 170 miles, 9,600 feet elevation and 11 and a half cycling hours.

It was so encouraging to be greeted by some friendly, familiar faces, especially Gary, who always gives me encouraging support. It is much appreciated. The supporters' coach arrived shortly after, and I could look forward to the game.

We had a disappointing first half, not helped by the horrible challenge of Allan Campbell deserving a red but somehow warranting a yellow. That was the end of the game as Campbell hobbled off and we were all hoping it wasn't a serious injury. To make matters worse, we conceded 2 goals to find ourselves behind at halftime – a frustrating half as there wasn't anything between the teams. A change of players and formation for the second half, it was encouraging to see Sonny Bradley and Luke Berry although I was resigned to a defeat.

However, we witnessed a brilliant comeback courtesy of 2 Luke Berry goals in the last 17 minutes in front of the Luton fans, including an equaliser in the 8$^{th}$ minute of added time. I was delighted for Luke, who had had his share of injury problems. Bezza always manages to find the spaces to create chances, and he has done it at every level for the club. It felt like a victory and I was buzzing at the end of the game. It was obvious what it meant to everyone, and we definitely enjoyed the journey home to rest and recover. Come on you Hatters!

# Wednesday 15th September at 7.45 pm - Bristol City

A quick turnaround from Blackburn which is normal for away games), but with a Wednesday game I had an extra 24 hours to prepare. Since Blackburn I had had a few days' rest and a Zone 2 cadence recovery ride to condition my legs for Bristol. Now, I had a friend, Paul, that I'd worked with at a previous company. He was a Bristol City fan and we'd made contact through Facebook. Now, back in the days we'd worked together, we were in the Conference, and they were in the Championship so we didn't have the rivalry banter. Anyway, we agreed we would meet up before the game. Paul was very kind to put me in touch with people who would promote my challenge – the guy who was responsible for the scoreboard and Ben who did online posts for Bristol City Football Club.

I was expecting the route to be approximately 115 miles, so I packed the night before and set off early at 6.18 am. Later that morning it was great to see a post from Luton Town along the lines of 'Whilst most Hatters fans are sleeping Mark is cycling to the game'. I had ridden the start of the route on training rides many times through Winslow and the Claydons out to Marsh Gibbon. Now with all my routes I have learned to expect the unexpected with road closures and the cycling app taking me on offroad routes going nowhere as was the case here and I ended up on the A41, which I followed to Kirtlington and Witney where I stopped at a cafe for a rest at about 47 miles and to give Paul an update.

There was a lot of activity on Twitter, with some motivational messages which really motivated me, not that I wasn't motivated before, but they really mean a lot and I try to reply to all of the messages when I can. The onward journey was uneventful apart from a few wrong turnings with steady elevation as I headed through Fairford towards Malmesbury, where I stopped for some lunch. I had completed 80 miles at this point, the temperature had risen significantly and it was in the 70s and warm. As it approached 1 pm, with my backpack and extra weight I was fatiguing and getting through my energy drinks, and I needed a break. I was making good time, so I made the most of a rest. Now attempting to get out of Malmesbury onto the right road became a challenge, with the navigation taking me down cobbled streets, over pedestrian bridges, along canals and generally round in circles for what seemed like about 20 minutes, but eventually I got back on track. The route took me through a number of villages but unfortunately road closures on my planned route meant a detour, and seeing signs to Chippenham and Bath I wasn't entirely confident I was on the right track as I passed over the M4 roundabout on a busy A road where I followed signs to Bath and turned off towards Bristol.

At this point I knew I had broken the back of the ride and found new energy levels for the final push to Ashton Gate. The last 10 miles were along busy roads in built-up areas as I was hitting rush hour traffic cycling through Kingswood and the suburbs of Bristol, St George, Lawrence Hill and finally along the river Avon, taking a shortcut through the park where I came out near the ground. I had finally arrived at Ashton Gate to complete Away Cycle Challenge 5: a total of 121 miles covered over 11 hours with 8 hours' cycling, 4,000 feet elevation and 2,700 calories burned.

Shortly after I arrived, I met Paul, and it was good to catch up and chat about the game. I was introduced to Ben, who interviewed me for the Bristol City online blog. It was enjoyable to chat to Ben, who is a credit to Bristol City. In addition, Stewart from the Bobbers Travel Club filmed me for a few words, and we had time to chat and have a few beers with supporters from both Luton Town and Bristol City. I was approached by a lady called Jess, who complimented me on my ride and told me of her dad, who was looked after by Keech Hospice. It really did have an impact on me how Keech helped people and that what I was doing was helping Keech Hospice.

Regarding the game, Bristol City hadn't won at home for 8 months, and we are usually good at helping teams/players break unwanted records, but we started on the front foot, chances came and went, the game should have been out of reach by halftime but was still 0-0. Against the run of play we fell behind to a set play early in the second half. The game was fading as we brought on Danny Hylton, with songs breaking out of 'When Hylton scores we're on the pitch'. Well, in the 91st minute, following an error from their keeper, Danny Hylton put it into an empty net for another late equaliser, and the Luton following went crazy – apart from a valuable away point, it was a significant moment to see Super Danny Hylton score his first goal in the championship. We had amassed 18 shots in the game so a draw was the very least we deserved. Come on you Hatters!

So, back on the coach for the journey home, another journey of heavy traffic and roadworks, such were the delays as the coach navigated onto the M25 and back to Luton. As a result, I got off the coach at 2 am, with a 45-minute cycle home, getting home just before 3 am and 21 hours after setting off from home. I was tired but it had been a great day. I managed 4 hours sleep before getting up for work – I had had 7 hours sleep in a 40-hour period, running on empty.

The Bristol City challenge really had a positive impact on the awareness and donations for the charities. From the day of the Bristol City game until the following weekend, I raised £560, bringing the total to £2,800, a staggering amount considering my original target was £3,000 and £1,000 for each charity.

# Saturday 25th September at 3 pm - Bournemouth

Away Cycle Challenge 6 to Bournemouth would be another cycle challenge spread over 2 days, with the first day to Totton near Southampton with a stop in Windsor at 42 miles to meet a friend, Stuart, for a catch-up. The route was familiar for the first 20 miles, at which point I checked my navigation and was shocked to see a message from ex- Luton player JJ O'Donnell, another 'wow' moment. The route took me through Wendover and High Wycombe into Marlow. After a break I set off again about 1 pm..

I seemed to be staying on fairly busy but direct roads as I bypassed Reading and headed south towards the region of Basingstoke, which was at the 70-mile mark. Now it was a warm, sunny day, which I wasn't complaining about, but fatigue had started to set in and I knew I needed to take in more fuel, especially as the elevation would rise for the rest of the ride. Direct roads are an opportunity to switch off the brain but also it's easy to lose concentration, which is not recommended, but I felt I was making progress. I approached Winchester at the 92-mile mark. I could start to cross off the miles knowing I had broken the back of the ride with only 16 miles to go, which was just as well as my legs were feeling tired.

Now I was approaching Totton and was a few miles from my destination – nice and straight-forward, no need to re-check the navigation – bad mistake! Instead of taking me on A roads it took me cross-country, through industrial estates, down cycle lanes, across fields, carrying the bike over walking gates and through a marsh onto a housing estate. It all added to the experience. Anyway, I arrived just before 7 pm, 11 hours after I had set off.

In total, 108 miles with 7 and a half hours' cycling time, 4,278 feet elevation and 2,700 calories burned. I booked into my Airbnb accommodation, which was perfect for what I needed to recover, and I had earned a meal and a few pints.

Due to the miles covered the day before, I had earned a lie-in, and as I only had just under 30 miles to get to Bournemouth, I set off just after 10.30 am.. The sunshine from the day before had disappeared and there was a forecast of rain. Now, not for the first time, navigating getting away from a built-up area was a challenge, but eventually I made it onto the road to Lyndhurst, taking the route to Christchurch. It was a ride that was kind to me and with very little elevation to cope with, I'm sure my legs appreciated it. I experienced some rain en route but it was comforting to know that after Christchurch I was only 7 to 8 miles from Bournemouth, arriving in good time, so I took the opportunity to go down to the seafront whilst looking for Hatters fans outside pubs.

The short ride on the Saturday was only 27 miles and took just under 2 hours' cycling time and I eventually made my way to the ground to offload my bike with the Bobbers Travel Club and bumped into Dan from Luton Town for a chat.

Away Cycle Challenge 6 had been completed and over 2 days I had cycled 135 miles with 9 and a half hours' cycling time with 5,000 feet elevation climbs and 3,500 calories burned.

Regarding the game, I didn't have high expectations. Bournemouth were riding high at the top of the league and for the first half looked every bit a promotion-hunting team. We weren't in the game and fell behind early, conceding a second goal on the half-hour mark – another game we'd started on the back foot.

To their credit, the heads didn't go down and there was a significant improvement in the second half, scoring just after the hour mark. Elijah Adebayo was involved in everything as we pushed for an equaliser. To be honest, Bournemouth were hanging on as we dominated, with Nathan making changes, but we couldn't force an equaliser and we went home disappointed but proud of the desire and commitment shown. It just shows how far the club is developing to be disappointed with a defeat to Bournemouth, but onto the next game, which would be a memorable 5-0 home win against Coventry City. Come on you Hatters!

This brought an end to September's away games and my challenges so with a few home games followed by another international break it was time to rest my legs. At the end of September an incredible £3,074 had been donated after 6 away games. When you think that this was my original target when I set out on the challenge, it is staggering and shows the generosity of everyone. Thank you, everyone!

# Saturday 16th October at 3 pm – Millwall

So, after another international break when I took the time to visit my family in Spain and get in some warm-weather cycling, it was back to Championship football, and it came as no surprise that there were 2 back-to-back away challenges. Now as soon as the fixtures were released, I nervously looked for the London away games, more out of dread than excitement as the thought of cycling in London filled me with nerves and trepidation.

Prior to the game, I contacted the Millwall Supporters through Twitter, and they were really supportive and agreed to put an article in the programme. It is really encouraging how the wider footballing community put aside rivalry to support worthwhile charities.

So, I started out at 7.30 am, with the weather forecast to be overcast but dry. I started on a familiar route out towards Whipsnade Zoo (a regular training route for some climbs) then out towards Markyate, Redbourn and then the busy A road to St Albans. Now I had said the forecast was to stay dry but the weather had other ideas and thought that I needed some challenging wet conditions. For a while there were signs of road closures into St Albans, another challenge, but luckily the footpaths were open, and I managed to reach the outskirts of St Albans at 18 miles.

The rain became heavier as I continued to London Colney, en route to South Mimms. I hadn't brought my overshoes, which would have kept my feet dry, and my gloves were soaked. This was my first soaking on my away challenges so for it to happen on Challenge 7, I should have counted myself lucky!

I arrived at South Mimms (services) and took refuge for a break from the rain and some protein and carbs refreshment. Now my navigation was getting confused so I had a tour of the services for a while before I engaged my brain and found the route into Barnet, which is where my London cycling experience would begin.

By this stage I had reached the 44-mile mark and had 17 miles to go and my worst fears didn't come to fruition as I stuck to the navigation route through traffic and along the North Circular briefly by Finchley, and down towards Kentish Town and Camden Town. By now, luckily, the rain had stopped, and I was making slow progress through the lunchtime traffic, where it was definitely an education seeing London cyclists' attitude to cycling in London.

At the 57-mile mark I passed over London Bridge and I knew that I was nearly there, just a few more miles, and I would arrive at the ground.

Away Cycle Challenge 7 was completed, a total of 61.5 miles, with a cycling time of 4 hours and 15 minutes in just over 5 hours with 2,136 feet elevation and 1,519 calories burned. Although it wasn't a demanding cycle, I think it was the stress of London cycling, which, however, wasn't as bad as I had feared.

So, because I had made good time, I arrived about 1 pm, and hung around the ground. I got my standard photo taken outside the ground and met a few people I had met at previous away games. I also had a really nice chat with Adrian Forbes, who arrived on his own. He was so friendly and approachable and was aware of what I was doing. As usual, I waited for the Bobbers Travel coach to arrive to offload my bike. Unfortunately, they were caught in traffic and didn't arrive until about 2.30pm but at least it stayed dry while I waited for them.

Now, we don't have a good track record in London and even less of a good record against Millwall, but today was an exceptional team performance and a thoroughly deserved win. We were on the front foot from the start and an excellent move finished with a quality Harry Cornick finish put us in front, cue the celebrations. The lead should have been more at half-time, but we need not have worried as it was doubled early in the second half by another Harry Cornick goal. Now, as convincing a performance as it was, Simon Sluga was in great form with some fine saves and none more so when Millwall won a penalty. Now despite our dominance, if they had scored it would have made for a nervous last 10 minutes, but Sluga made a great penalty save and we won 2-0. I, along with the other Hatters fans, was buzzing, a great away win.

Back on the coach for a happy journey home, and all that was left was my final cycle home from Flitwick after departing the coach. I arrived home just after 9 pm. – In total I had cycled 785 miles to the 7 away games. I was looking forward to a lazy Sunday.

# Tuesday 19th October at 7.45 pm - Derby County

Another short turnaround for Away Cycle Challenge 8 to Derby County. It had now become a bit of a routine of back-to-back away games. Since the Millwall game, I had rested up with an indoor training session the day before to spin my legs with low intensity. Now, I pay a lot of attention to weather forecasts to plan for routes and specifically what I should wear, and the forecast for my Derby ride was heavy rain all day and strong winds, so out came the waterproof jackets, gloves, overshoes and extra protection for the change of clothes I was carrying. I also took bike number 2, which was the Planet X, my entry-level bike that comes out in winter to cope with the bad weather.

Luckily, I started off in dry conditions; however, the weather forecast was correct with the windy conditions. Now, the difference between the Planet X and the Trek Emonda (apart from the cost) is the weight, along with the extra weight of carrying about 6kg behind the saddle and on my back so in the windy conditions it was a challenging ride, especially as I hadn't been on the Planet X for a few months. The first ride back on the Planet X is like comparing a tractor to a sports car, which doesn't last long. My other mistake was fitting a new saddle beforehand without trying it out, which was highlighted later in the ride.

So, I set off about 10.30 am for a journey that was expected to be around 75 miles, and as with the previous northern rides, I started with navigating around Northampton through Duston, Althorp and on quiet roads in the direction of Lutterworth. At this point I had cycled 38 miles and was halfway, still avoiding rain at this point.

Remember my earlier comment about testing a new saddle before a long ride? Well, it came loose but I managed to get to Coalville at 62 miles when I found a Costa next to a Halfords – perfect! Anyway, they tightened the saddle in the wrong position but at least I only had 17 miles to go, and as far as the route was concerned, it was fairly straightforward and uneventful. The last 5 miles were all on cycle paths, navigating bikes, pedestrians and prams – as a rule I try to avoid cycle paths and keep to main roads, unless it is too dangerous. I find I lose the momentum on cycle paths and tend to pick up more punctures.

I had been to Pride Park a few times but as I approached the ground on cycle paths it didn't dawn on me how close I was to the ground until I got about half a mile away when I could see Pride Park. Away Cycle Challenge 8 was completed in 79 miles and just under 5 and a half hours' cycling time with 3,700 feet elevation and 2,600 calories burned.

Prior to this cycle challenge, I had messaged the Derby County Twitter pages to see if they would retweet it. It's interesting, the perception of clubs that you think would be supportive and those that are not, and Derby were brilliant, with retweets, encouraging messages and generous donations. Genuine, sincere football fans will support great causes regardless of what's going on with their own club.

The game itself was in stark contrast to the impressive win at Millwall. We were off the pace from the start. Derby had a higher intensity and went behind after 20 minutes but got to half-time with no further goals and with changes at half-time they came out for the second half more like the Luton team of a few days ago. They had made the perfect start to the second half with Fred Onyedinma scoring, and the saying of 'goals change games' was very true when Derby retook the lead on the hour and the momentum changed again. We managed to build pressure near the end and managed to get another late equaliser with an Elijah Adebayo header. Whenever we score late to rescue a point it always feels like a win despite not being at our best, great qualities to grind out results and those battling away points will be vital at the end of the season. It was a happy journey home with a point. Come on you Hatters!

G
DERBY COUNTY FOOTBALL CLUB
The Lionel Pickering Entrance

# Saturday 30th October at 3 pm - Preston North End

It had been 10 days since the Derby County challenge ride, time which I had spent resting and ticking over with indoor Zwift rides and a 56-mile weekend following the home game against Hull City. By comparison, without an away game, the activity on the donation page and social media was quiet although this would change massively in the build-up to the long trip to Preston North End. Whilst I was cycling to Derby County, I received a message from Jon at BBC Look East, wanting to run a piece about my challenge on the evening news programme and after several great conversations it was agreed that I would be filmed with action shots and interviewed from my home before I set off on my 2-day cycle to Preston North End.

The interviewer/cameraman arrived about 7.45 am., He was very friendly, and this relaxed me. Normally, having too much time to think about interviews for my challenge makes me very self-conscious and nervous – how will I come across? Will I say the wrong thing? Fortunately, on this occasion, I didn't really have time to be nervous with my focus being taken up with preparing for my 2-day cycle challenge. The pre-set questions which were explained to me beforehand to help me relax were around my challenge. Why was I doing the challenge? And also about Mick Harford, Luton Town and the season so far and aspirations for the season ahead. I thought it went ok whilst at the time I was still self-critical . The cameraman was conscious of the time so wrapped up the interview and went outside for action shots of me leaving the house and setting off on my bike, trying to make it realistic with several retakes. The first time was me coming out of the house, leaving the front door open and cycling off, not very realistic! So, he filmed some action shots of me cycling and on one occasion made an amusing comment that I was cycling too fast for the video, amusing because I have never been told I'm cycling too fast! Anyway, after about half an hour of action shots the cameraman was happy with the video and we said our goodbyes, he left, and I made my final preparations for departing for my challenge to Preston.

The second part of the BBC interview was that they wanted to do a live interview when I arrived in Leek. The ride on the Friday was going to be approximately 110 miles so I had the added pressure of arriving in time to do the interview but I had time as this would be about 6.30 pm, so I set off from home at 8.45 am. The interviews meant an additional 6 miles from where I usually set off from in Newport Pagnell. I was familiar with the route as I had taken a similar route to Blackburn. The route went to Blackburn, Preston and

Blackpool, traffic and road closures permitting. The weather forecast was for intermittent rain showers, so I dressed prepared.

So I headed on my usual route through Northampton, arriving at Lutterworth at the 45-mile mark. Now, normally I look to stop for a break at the 3-hour point but I felt quite good so I decided to push on and take a break when the heavy rain came so I could take shelter. At this point, although the rain was light and occasional it wasn't anything that would soak me. What usually happens is that I put the waterproofs on and the rain stops, I take them off and it starts again – sod's law! So, not finding another café I had to make do with a break at a garden centre for some protein bars and a drink and to check my phone for messages. I was getting a lot of donations and encouraging messages, which always gives me a lift to get through the day, so with added motivation, I progressed through Market Bosworth and arrived at Burton-on-Trent at the 80-mile mark. My experience from my Blackburn ride was that around the 90-mile mark the elevation would get tougher for the remainder of the day's cycling, so at least I was prepared this time. Only a tough 25 miles to go for the day.

By now I had a message from BBC Look East that they wanted to test the zoom link at 5.30 pm, which meant I had to have a big push. I climbed through the Uttoxeter area and took a flat route on busy roads for the last 6 miles to make up the time. I eventually arrived at my accommodation in Leek just after 5 pm. . On the whole, I had been lucky with the weather but wouldn't be so lucky for the final journey the next day to Preston.

My Day 1 of the cycle challenge to Preston was 115 miles with 7 hours 47 minutes of cycling time and a demanding 5,761 feet elevation, burning just over 3,000 calories.

The zoom testing for the second part of my BBC interview took place about 6 pm, with the administrator trying to get me to change settings on my phone. Now, I'm not a technical person and even less after cycling all day but it got sorted in time and I had time to look presentable and the interview went well and was finished just before 7 pm, which left the evening to rest and recover with a pub meal and a few well-deserved pints of cider.

My Day 2 cycle challenge from Leek to Preston will go down as one of the toughest days of the challenge, mostly due to the conditions. It was 68 miles in total, the B & B wasn't serving breakfast when I was ready to leave, and just as the heavy rain started, the ride up to Macclesfield took me by the edge of the Peak District and I had some aggressive climbs. The 10 miles to Macclesfield were at 1,600-feet elevation in heavy rain, with legs still tired from the previous day's cycling – definitely character-building. Half the climbs of the 68 miles came in the first 10 miles, and the rain eased slightly as I approached Sale and Stretford and cycled through Trafford Park Shopping Centre. The rest from the rain didn't last long as I passed the Bolton Wanderers ground, and by this stage I had cycled 48 miles for the day, I was cold and wet and I wanted the fastest route to Preston regardless of the traffic, not the most sensible choice but I just wanted the ride over.

My next checkpoint was Chorley at 58 miles, only 10 miles to go. Surely, I had seen the last of the rain for the day – wrong again, the biggest downpour was saved for the final part of the journey, when even the navigation stopped working. Because of the challenges of the ride and the conditions, I didn't arrive at Deepdale until about 2.15 pm, 6 hours after I had left Leek and without breakfast but at least I had completed Away Cycle Challenge 11. Over the 2 days, I had cycled 183 miles with nearly 13 hours of cycling, with 8,800 feet elevation and over 6,000 calories burned, and the total had now passed the 1,000 mile mark. All that was required was to have my usual photo taken outside the ground and find the coach and change into some alternative clothes – fortunately some of them had stayed dry during my rides, partly due to the packaging. I then checked my phone for the messages of support and the generous donations.

Now, after my adventures getting to Deepdale, I was hoping for an encouraging performance to make the journey worthwhile, but unfortunately, it was a disappointing performance that didn't offer anything in terms of creativity and scoring opportunities. We had the benefit of a few extra days' rest with Preston having a Carabao Cup game against Liverpool, but we fell behind just before the half-hour mark with the big talking point of the goal being: did he mean to shoot or was it a cross? Getting to halftime only 1-0 down would have been an achievement, but unfortunately, in the first half's injury time, we conceded a penalty which was converted so 2-0 behind at halftime and the second half, despite changes to line-up and formation, was mostly forgettable with no change to the score. I remember a comment on social media that made me smile, someone said that the team had played like they had all cycled to Preston North End!

Anyway, it was back on the coach with the difficult task of choosing a Man of the Match and I made the journey home thanks to the Bobbers Travel Club.

The Preston game had seen the completion of my away cycle challenges in October with the cumulative donations raised approaching £3,700, an incredible amount that I was extremely grateful for.

Time for a rest with another international break before the next away game.

# Friday 19th November at 7.45 pm- Queens Park Rangers

This fixture is one of the first I look out for when the fixture lists come out mainly because my best friend of over 30 years is a passionate QPR supporter, not that there is much banter with our terrible record – we hadn't won at QPR since 1984, when I was there as an 18- year-old. Our record at home isn't much better, so I didn't have high expectations, especially as QPR were doing well in the Championship. Now, the game was originally planned for Saturday until Sky moved the game to a Friday night for TV. I wasn't overly impressed at the thought of cycling through London rush-hour traffic on a Friday evening.

This game came after another international break, when I had taken the opportunity to visit my sister and family in Tampa. It was nice to meet up and get some relaxation in warmer weather. On my return, I nervously took my COVID test, which fortunately came back negative so I could proceed with plans for the QPR away trip.

I planned the route and decided to cycle to Luton Town's ground on my way to say hello to anyone that was there and hopefully get some photos taken inside the ground. Now, usually I like to wake up hours before I leave and have time for a relaxing few hours, but on this occasion, I also had to take the bike to a shop for adjustments to the saddle. The one time I had a busy preparation, I slept in and didn't wake up until 9.30 am, so it was a stressed, hectic runaround getting the bike sorted, final packing, having some breakfast and I got on my way just after 11 am., As I had made the journey to Kenilworth Road on hundreds of occasions over 40 years, I could switch my brain to auto-pilot whilst I regained my composure en route to the ground and I made the 19-mile journey, arriving just before 12.30.

The response I received from Janet and Lisa on reception was brilliant and after a chat I had some photos taken outside the Mick Harford Billboard and then I was taken inside the ground for some nice photos. This was probably my only opportunity to get some bike photos inside the ground. I then spent some time with the team in the ticket office for a chat and after some social media posts I carried on with my journey around 1 pm..

From Luton, I left the town centre and joined the busy dual carriageway to Harpenden and the short ride into St Albans, at which point I had cycled 21 miles. From this point it was a fairly uneventful cycle to Elstree at 40 miles, and now there were just under 14 miles to go but it was about 2.30 pm at this time and I knew I would be hitting London traffic soon.

My next checkpoint was Edgware, which was where my navigation took place. I should have gone through Edgware and taken a route in a built-up area with less of the hectic traffic. Instead, I ended up on the busy dual carriageway A41 /A1 through Hendon and Brent Cross, attempting to navigate the traffic through to Cricklewood at the 48-mile mark. Although the remaining 6 miles were in built-up traffic with frustrating red-light stops, it was straightforward following the navigation map and I finally arrived at the ground just before 4.30 pm.

I had completed Away Cycle Challenge 10, cycling 54 miles in 3 hours 49 minutes with a steady 1,900 feet elevation.

My good friend John had travelled down early to meet me and after taking photos and changing, we found a Starbucks to warm up and get food and a warm drink. John had gone to a lot of trouble to write an article about my challenge for the QPR fanzine only to find out they hadn't put it in the programme for the game. In addition, none of the QPR supporters' Twitter pages had retweeted details of my challenge. Very frustrating, but unfortunately, that wouldn't be the biggest frustration of the evening.

About 7 pm, I decided to go into the ground, although finding the entrance to the upper tier was a challenge, although nothing in comparison to the problems some supporters had gaining entry with some in a queue for 45 minutes.

Regarding the game, as I mentioned previously, I didn't have high expectations, due to our form against QPR but we did make a promising start and created chances early in the game with Elijah Adebayo having a great opportunity and during the positive start we won a corner. Unfortunately, we were caught on the break and a clinical finish found us behind, but we were still looking threatening. We went into half time 1-0 behind. I was still positive we could get something from the game and we created more chances at the beginning of the second half but were caught again, and, no surprise, went 2-0 behind to Charlie Austin, who always scores against us! The remainder of the game was largely uneventful and finished with us losing again to QPR.

If I thought that would be the end of the drama, I would sadly be mistaken. Now, I have followed Luton Town away over 40 years but the experience after leaving the ground was one of the worst. Firstly, both sets of supporters were allowed to leave the ground at the same time. Now, my route back to the coach was to turn right out of the ground and the coach was parked down a side street, a 5-minute walk away. However, the police had blocked the route and we were forced to turn left. I expected to make a left turn eventually to make my way back to the ground to find the coach, but all the roads were blocked and as I found myself on Uxbridge Road the atmosphere was extremely hostile.

Unknown at the time, there was someone lying in the road and later I would find out that a Luton fan had been attacked and would be rushed to hospital with life-threatening injuries and placed in a coma. No one should ever go to a football game and end up in hospital in a coma – this was like football trouble in the eighties.

On a number of occasions I stopped and asked police officers for directions back to the coach, but they were no help, it was like a 'not my problem' attitude and I was left on my own to find a way back. My experience of the police at away games over the years has been positive, friendly, helpful, and respectful, but it was the complete opposite on this occasion. At this point, I had passed Shepherd's Bush station and I was panicking that I would miss the coach so I decided to walk back in the direction I had come from, right back to the exit of the stadium, where at this point, the crowd had left and the road was open to find my way back to the coach.

On return to the coach, I found that I wasn't the only person that had experienced this and there were people phoning from White City tube station that were lost and couldn't find their way back to the coach – this should never happen. The coach eventually left the ground just before 10.30 pm, an hour after the game finished. I really hope that I don't have to go back there again soon.

Because of the delay leaving the ground, it was midnight before the coach got back to Flitwick, where I set off on my 11-mile cycle back home, eventually arriving just before 1 am, a long and frustrating day but at least I had completed another challenge and I had the rest of the weekend to recover.

## Tuesday 23rd November at 7.45 pm – Nottingham Forest

Following a rest day after my QPR excursions, I took in a ride on the Sunday. With cold temperatures forecast the coming week, I thought I would get in a cold weather training ride with Andy, who had volunteered to join me on the Swansea trip, so I did a 3 and a half-½ hour ride of just over 50 miles. Now the temperature was officially 4 degrees but felt colder so it was good preparation and nice to catch up with Andy and I rested on the Monday prior to the Nottingham Forest ride.

Now, the Nottingham ride preparation in a northern direction began much like previous rides – getting the bike ready and packed with bags the night before, an early breakfast and preparing myself for a cold ride before driving to Newport Pagnell at 9 am to leave my car for my return. On my final checks, I noticed the front tyre wasn't as pumped as it had appeared the night before. I tried to inflate it without success, so rather than fixing it on the roadside, I walked into a bike shop in Newport Pagnell, where the staff were very helpful and replaced the inner tube, which had a leaking valve. Although an inconvenience, this was Away Cycle 11 and my first mechanical issue so I couldn't really complain when my start was delayed until about 10.15 am.

This route would be very familiar to my cycle to Barnsley earlier in the season but a lot colder. The temperature on my Garmin didn't get higher than 37 degrees fahrenheit, as I headed out to Northampton, navigating the traffic through Kingsthorpe. At this point, I picked up the A5199at the 20-mile mark with the first checkpoint being Chapel Brampton. Now my experience from the Barnsley ride was that the A5199 route was a long straightish route to Wigston in Leicestershire for about 23 miles. The benefit of this road was that I could switch off my brain and push out the miles but unlike on the previous ride this one was extremely cold with no real checkpoints. This section seemed to last forever, the miles countdown seemed to freeze just like the weather and the pace seemed really slow. The main reason for focusing on Wigston was that there was a Costa to take a break and get warm again. I reached this point at 43 miles.

The benefit of doing several rides in the same direction is that I can learn from previous experience and previously I had had to face busy dual carriageways on the Leicester bypass, so this time I decided to cycle through Leicester, stopping at every traffic light or so it seemed, and this was at about 2 pm so I hit the traffic. After escaping the traffic, I headed out to Mountsorrel at 55 miles and I had broken the back of the journey with only 17 miles to go. The route took me through a number of villages on fairly uneventful roads with moderate traffic, and when I reached Ruddington at 68 miles I knew I was nearly there, which was just as well as the light was starting to fade. This route would avoid the busy Nottingham traffic until I reached the West Bridgford area, and as I got closer the built-up area became familiar from my trips to the area for international cricket at Trent Bridge and I eventually reached the ground at 4.15 pm.

Away Cycle Challenge 11 was achieved, at 72 miles with just under 5 hours' cycling time and 3,000 feet elevation. After my usual photo outside the ground, I now had a few hours spare waiting for Bobbers Coach to arrive. Prior to the winter months, I had decided it was better to arrive in daylight and have a few hours spare rather than navigating rush hour traffic in the dark. The challenge was somewhere to leave the bike. The NFFC ticket office wouldn't help, and Wetherspoon's Trent Bridge Inn also wasn't prepared to let me keep the bike inside but luckily I found a pub opposite the ground which let me put my bike in the corner as I was only staying for 40 minutes. Anyway, after catching up with Luke from 'Oh when the town' podcast it was a few hours before I left the pub and found the coach to get into the ground just before kick-off.

The game was largely uneventful, as the 0-0 score line suggests, although we seemed more likely to win on the very few chances created, with the best chance around the hour mark when we were awarded a penalty and as a result, Forest were reduced to 10 men. Now, Elijah Adebayo is usually so reliable with penalties but on this occasion, the keeper saved it and got away with moving off his goal line before the kick was taken. With Forest down to 10 men, it became harder to break them down. They sat deep and no significant chances were created. James Shea, who came into the side, kept a clean sheet and had a solid game; he never lets us down. A point away from home is a positive result, and despite Forest's attacking options they didn't have an attempt on target, although we left the ground feeling disappointed, a good sign of our progression especially with Forest's recent improved form.

This was the final away cycle for November and I had raised £375 that month, making a total of just over £4,000, such amazing generosity. Post-Forest and before the next away game at Blackpool, my focus was on setting up a new Just Giving donation page due to Virgin Money Giving closing on 30$^{th}$ November. The Bobbers Travel Club were brilliant in supporting this change, especially Stewart and Kevin.

# Saturday 4th December at 3 pm – Blackpool

As there was a home game in the week before the Blackpool game, I had the rare luxury of 10 days' recovery following the Nottingham Forest game, with a home game against Cardiff City (and the return of James Collins) over the weekend. I did a steady 43-mile ride to keep my legs ticking over in preparation for the long Blackpool ride.

Now, the night before preparation was a lot different to all of the previous challenges, as I was attending the Luton Town Christmas dinner. On arrival and checking in, I was greeted by 'Oh, you're the cyclist' and the first person that I met was Gary Sweet and we had a nice chat. Now, this was the first Luton Town Christmas dinner that I had attended and I didn't really know anyone but I found my table and looked forward to the evening.

The evening started with a 'Who wants to be a millionaire' style competition, which I failed miserably and bombed out on the first-round question – who is taller, Christian Walton or Elijah Adebayo? (for those interested it was Christian Walton by one inch at 6 foot 5 inches). Anyway, the competition was won by a lady called Lindsay, who donated the prize money to charity and Gary Sweet announced to everyone it should go to my challenge charities, a fantastic gesture and after that everyone knew me and the conversations flowed all evening, including a brief chat with Nathan Jones, and a few ex-players and it was a massive lift to receive compliments for my challenge from heroes of mine. I was loving the evening and although I knew I had an early start and a long day's cycling the next day, I didn't want the evening to end but I eventually left just before 12.30 am, getting home just after 1 am.

Due to work commitments, I hadn't prepacked for the cycle challenge so by the time that I had finished packing I finally got to bed about 2.30 am for some sleep before a long 3 days of cycling to Blackpool.

Away Cycle Challenge 12 was a planned 190-mile cycle over 3 days, which would be the longest challenge of the season to date, with some really tough weather conditions forecasted. Day 1 was a 80-mile cycle to just past Burton-on-Trent; with the temperature being brutally cold; the day's ride was a real struggle with temperatures barely rising above freezing and with the wind chill it felt like minus 5 degrees. A main challenge of cycling in freezing temperatures is the body having to work harder, depleting energy levels and taking into account I had only got 3 and a half hours' sleep it required mental strength as much as physical effort. The route was a familiar one as I headed north through Northampton and Lutterworth into Leicestershire, where I took a break at the 40-mile mark, and found a Costa to try and warm up, especially my fingers, and I treated myself to a slice of millionaire shortbread! I knew I had reached halfway, and when the conditions are challenging, I break down the ride into 5-mile segments and don't look too far ahead, and it helps to focus the mind on staying positive.

Having completed the north-west rides to Preston and Blackburn, it helped to have an idea of what was ahead as I made my way towards Market Bosworth and some familiar villages en route. At this point I was 25 miles from finishing the day but such was the temperature, my protein bars had frozen and I wasn't getting my protein nutrition to repair muscle tissue and delay the fatigue process. However, I reached Burton-on-Trent at 75 miles with only 5 miles to go, which was just as well as I was losing all feeling in the end of my fingers and the light was fading so it required a final push to finish.

Day 1 of Away Cycle Challenge 12 was completed – 80 miles in total, with nearly 4,000 feet elevation and just under 6 hours of cycling time. Fortunately, I had booked into a hotel with an onsite bar and restaurant, and they were very helpful with storing my bike, which is a prerequisite of my accommodation bookings. The evening was spent resting, recovering, eating and keeping warm.

Because of my prior knowledge of the route, I knew that Day 2, although it would be the same distance, would be brutally tough climbs, so at least I was prepared for what lay ahead. The temperature was a few degrees warmer, which to be honest wasn't difficult, but it still wasn't a comfortable temperature. However, the challenges made me even more determined.

As I cycled through Staffordshire on the edge of the New Forest and Peak District, I had to navigate 37 miles of really tough climbs before the route was less demanding on my legs. I was also having to navigate the tricky road conditions, and because of the freezing conditions, some of the descents were very scary and in some places I was afraid to touch the brakes in case I hit black ice and risked coming off. As hard as the climbs were, I actually felt safer than the descents, which added to the poor visibility. It wasn't a fun ride so staying focused, concentrating and not letting my mind wander were all really important.

The peak of the climbs took me to the 37-mile mark with 3,500 feet elevation, which gives an indication of the challenges of the first half of the day. Due to the difficulties at this stage, it had taken me just over 3 hours and I was behind schedule, but I was fatiguing .and needed to take a break. Experience had taught me to take the rest, as it is counter-productive to keep going when the mind and body are tired and cold so I had a break to recharge the batteries when I reached Macclesfield and some treats from a coffee shop. I rely on finding coffee shops that let me bring my bike inside, and it was also an opportunity to recharge my Garmin and light appliances.

The second half of the day's ride, although less demanding, brought its own challenges. I had left the climbs behind and now had to navigate traffic through Sale and the outskirts of Manchester as I passed through Trafford Park to Worsley. At this point, I had reached 65 miles and although I had only 15 miles to go, the light was fading quickly and realised I would be arriving in the dark so I took the decision to take a direct route which was quicker but on busy 'A' roads, and eventually, I arrived in the Chorley area at Adlington.. I had completed Day 2, another really tough day on the bike.

Day 2 had been completed, cycling 80 miles with over 4,500 feet elevation and although it was just over 6 hours' cycling time, it was much longer due to the climbs earlier in the day and the traffic in built-up areas. It felt like I had stopped at every traffic light!

The accommodation had been found on Airbnb and was in a nice location, very helpful with the bike. Unfortunately, it wasn't a good location to get a meal, either booked-up pubs or just takeaways, and a curry isn't the ideal recovery meal to bulk up on carbs so after walking what seemed like mile after mile, I settled for a Tesco meal deal, not ideal, but a common theme of the event is to adjust to the challenges faced and I rested up for the final Day 3 of the cycle to Blackpool.

At the end of each day, it is so rewarding and inspiring to read all the messages of support and encouragement, which give me a huge lift, especially at times when my spirits are flagging, and my positivity isn't always where it needs to be. It helps me to focus why I'm doing this challenge, which is motivational and helps me to re-focus on the tasks ahead. It was time to rest, recover and recharge the batteries.

As I rested up before the final day of the 3-day cycle challenge to Blackpool, my mindset was that the hard work was done – 2 days of 80 miles on each day with only just over 30 miles to complete with undemanding ascents, so although the weather forecast was for rain, I didn't take the day's cycling too seriously after the previous 2 days, and expected an easy day's cycling before seeing the game. This taught me a valuable lesson not to take any day's cycling on this challenge for granted.

So, after a light breakfast supplied by my Airbnb host, I set off with a pre-arranged stop after just 7 miles to catch up with my friend Lois. After about an hour, I set off with only 25 miles to go. However, the weather became more challenging, the rain became heavier and the wind became stronger. I reached the outskirts of Preston at the 11-mile mark. My pre-planned route was to follow the coastal route to Lytham and Lytham St Annes along the promenade into Blackpool, but at the point the conditions got significantly worse. In hindsight, I should have been flexible in my plans and headed inland to save a battering from the winds but I was too stubborn, another lesson learned. The last 20 miles was one of the most challenging rides, and I was soaked from the driving rain and getting battered from the winds from Lytham and for the last 7 miles I must have averaged 10mph. All my effort was focussed on keeping the bike upright, having to stop on a number of occasions to regain my focus and composure. Even as I approached Blackpool and came off the promenade towards the ground, I was trying to avoid falling over and making collisions with other vehicles. Anyway, to my relief, I finally arrived at the ground.

Away Cycle Challenge 12 had been achieved – 193 miles across 3 days, freezing temperatures, wind, rain and over 9,200 feet elevation. It had been easily the toughest of the challenges so far.

I took shelter in the reception at the ground to get out of the wind and after a few minutes, I was greeted by Gary Sweet and David Wilkinson, who were very supportive, giving their time to make sure that I was ok, and wanting to help me with anything I needed. Firstly, they asked if I needed any warm clothes, and I only mentioned that I didn't know if my spare clothes would be dry from my ride and they arranged for a winter coat and training kit to change into, with Gary offering for me to call him if there was anything else I needed. So, after changing, I was offered to take up my match ticket seat or join Gary and David in the director's box, so after getting my bike on the coach, I decided to take them up on their generous offer. I expected this to be a one-off opportunity.

As well as the opportunity to get warm and be fed in hospitality, it was an absolute pleasure to be in the company of Gary and David. They were so friendly, generous and genuinely interested in me and I felt so relaxed in their company — we are all so lucky to have such amazing people running our club, who have only the best interests of the club and the community at heart. The Blackpool directors and officials were also friendly and supportive.

So I watched the game with Gary and David from the comfort of the director's area. It was still brutally cold, although if it was cold watching it must have been so much tougher playing in driving rain and hurricane-type conditions. In the earlier exchanges Blackpool adapted better and Sheasy made several brilliant saves to keep us in the game. We managed to get a foothold in the game and took the lead in the final minute of the first half through our man-mountain, Sonny Bradley, to go in 1-0 up at halftime. After warming up in the hospitality with Gary and David, I was further warmed up when Adebayo doubled our lead early in the second half the result wasn't in doubt and a late Jordan Clark goal was the icing on the cake, to seal a dominant win. I went back to the sanctuary of the warmth to say my goodbyes to Gary and David and made my way back to the coach. The memories of the Blackpool challenge and the support and encouragement I received will stay with me forever.

Regarding the charity donations, the weekend of the Blackpool game had raised £325, taking the total donations to just under £4,500, an incredible amount considering this was the halfway mark of the away games.

# COVID-19 and a month without football

On Saturday 11th December we watched an entertaining, exciting game against promotion-chasing Fulham, getting a 1-1 deserved draw which could have been more against a team worth millions. Little did we know at the time, it would be the last game played by Luton Town for a month until the FA cup game on Sunday 9th January 2022 due to COVID-19 affecting cancellations of games. We had been here before, it was a case of déjà vu!

This had a big impact on my away cycle challenge, and the first one to be cancelled was the trip to Reading planned for 16th December so with a free weekend I got in a couple of rides as, at the time, I still had a busy Christmas/New Year with trips to Swansea City and Coventry City.

The next announcement came late evening on the 20th of December, that all games played in Wales would be played without any fans. Now, such was my determination to cycle to all away games, it didn't enter my mind not to cycle to the game, so my focus turned to how I would get home from the game that I wouldn't be able to watch. I didn't sleep much that night.

The next morning, I got a message from Gary Sweet saying they were looking at ways I could be inside the stadium to watch the game, followed by a conversation with Stu Hammond. Incredibly, they had got me a media pass and even more amazing, I would be joining Simon Pitts on commentary, a once-in-a-lifetime experience. The club are truly incredible, how many other clubs would have gone to the lengths they did to help me? They really do care about their supporters, the community as well as the club, and we are so lucky to have such brilliant people running the club.

Unfortunately, on Christmas Eve, I got a message from Gary that the game would be cancelled, again due to COVID-19. I was gutted and really upset, the opportunity to experience this would probably not happen again; furthermore, the Boxing Day game for which I had been kindly offered a hospitality experience, was also cancelled, this time due to COVID-19 in the Luton Town team, and again, the away trip to Coventry City was cancelled for the same reason – frustrating but not surprising.

Although I didn't realise it at the time, the cancelled games were a blessing as on Boxing Day I trapped a nerve in my back. Considering the miles I had cycled up to that point, I had been lucky to avoid back injuries so I thought that it would be fine in a couple of days. How wrong I was!

I began treatment on 30th December, and initially had an adverse reaction, which resulted in not being able to move from bed without a lot of pain. I had more treatment 5 days later, and by this stage it had been announced that the Reading fixture had been rescheduled for 19th January so I had exactly 2 weeks for my back to get fixed to allow the away cycle challenge to continue, as not cycling to Reading wasn't an option. An easy indoor 45-minute ride on the 8th January proved painful, and at this stage my back was increasingly becoming a concern. With further treatment sessions, my back started to improve but I was advised not to cycle at all until the day before Reading to avoid making the injury worse, so I spent nearly 2 weeks in physio sessions, resting, stretching exercises with a couple of home games to watch in the build-up to Reading away. However, I wasn't thinking of my back during the celebrations at the dramatic end to the Bournemouth game courtesy of the 97th minute Kal Naismith winner – wow, what an incredible game, I was buzzing for days afterwards. Come on you Hatters!

# Wednesday 19th January 2022 at 8 pm – Reading

So, after 47 days of away cycle challenge inactivity, it was back on the road for the ride to Reading, feeling excited to be cycling to another away game but extremely nervous to see how my back would respond to 4 hours plus in the saddle. The previous 2 weeks had been spent building up to the next 4 days!

A massive help for me was that Stu and the media team agreed to take my rucksack to Reading for me which saved me carrying 3 kg on my back. Everyone at LTFC is incredible how they help and support me so much.

I decided to make an early start of just after 10 am for a 4-to-5-hour ride just in case I needed regular rest breaks. The first 15 minutes was on a familiar route that I had cycled many times on training rides, so it was nice to relax into the ride and not have to concentrate on navigation. I decided to take the same route through Wendover and High Wycombe to Marlow as I had for the Bournemouth trip, although I wasn't confident enough to make the journey without navigation. I arrived at Marlow at 38 miles at about 1 pm. My legs were starting to feel tired and I needed a rest to recover, with the first sign of 2 weeks of inactivity catching up with me. Now, I would like to say my recovery is all about carbs and protein fluid replacement, which it is some of the time, but as I find a Costa my eyes are first fixed on a big slice of millionaire shortbread. I just can't resist!

Now, it was 1.30 pm and I had only 20 miles to go. My back hadn't given me any problems at all so I didn't need a rest up until Marlow. The route out of Marlow required a section of a busy dual carriageway to Reading; sometimes it is easier to take a direct route for a short distance although can be a bit scary. Anyway, I got back on the quieter roads which take longer but are safer, took a few wrong turnings en route to Reading but I was comfortable that I had plenty of time and I eventually arrived at the ground around 3.30 pm for an 8 pm kick-off. I had completed Away Cycle Challenge 13, cycling 58 miles for just under 4 and a half hours. To my relief, my back hadn't caused me any issues.

After my usual photo outside of the ground, I was fortunate that Reading had a hotel on site, so I parked the bike outside reception and relaxed with a cider. It wasn't long afterwards that I received a call from Stu to say he had arrived with my warm clothes. Now, I hadn't brought my big coat, but Stu had a spare coat with him. Stu really does look after me when I arrive at the grounds. After getting changed in the hotel toilets, I got another message that the coach had arrived. It was only 5.30 and I wasn't the only one to arrive early, but it is always nice to see the coach arrive so I can offload the bike and get ready for the game.

Before the game, I had time to feed myself at a local McDonald's in a retail park, and I was joined by Mike, who is one of several supporters of my challenge and we regularly meet up at away games.

I made my way into the ground for the game along with 900 other Hatters fans. Now, this game came 4 days after the incredible Bournemouth win and Nathan Jones kept the same time apart from one change with Peter Kioso coming in for James Bree. Elijah Adebayo was a constant threat and we were creating down the flanks so it came as no surprise that we scored starting from a good build-up and were crossed by Jordan Clark for an own goal for the second time in a week, all gifts gratefully accepted! It was a game where we never felt threatened and we doubled our lead through Allan Campbell, with another outstanding performance being rewarded by a second goal just before the hour mark. As a fan following the Hatters we are usually guarding against the comeback, which here never materialised, and we comfortably held on for the win. We were really building momentum in the middle of a busy period, hoping we could keep it going for now, then travelling home in a happy mood celebrating a win. Come on you Hatters!

As with all the southern games, I had the cycle home from Flitwick, where the coach dropped me off just after midnight and I eventually got home just before 1 am, tired but very happy. Come on you Hatters!

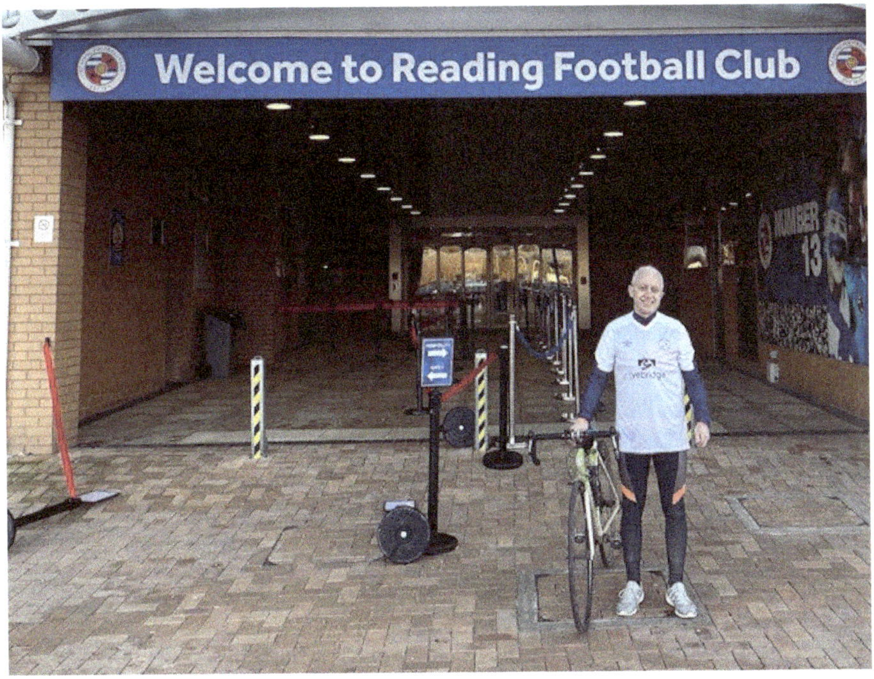
Welcome to Reading Football Club

# Saturday 22nd January 2022 at 3 pm – Sheffield United

So if you count my cycle home from Flitwick for the Reading game at 12.08 am as a Thursday cycle, then I had no recovery time before I started my Away Cycle Challenge 14 to Sheffield United. The morning started with my bag dropped off at Luton Town FC, with a brief chat with Dan before I drove to Newport Pagnell to drop off my car and prepare to set off on a 2-day cycle to Sheffield just before 10.30 am.

It was going to be another cold ride. I started in temperatures of 1 degree, which felt like minus 3 with the wind chill. The route planned was for approximately 80 miles to Hucknall for my stopover. The route would take me along a very similar route as the Forest game – through Northampton, picking up the A5199 road to Wigston just outside Leicester. To take my mind off the cold weather, I was counting in 5-mile segments. As I mentioned previously, looking too far ahead on the day's cycling can be mentally draining (if 5 hours plus cycling in the cold isn't hard enough). Anyway, I reached Wigston at the 45-mile mark, where I attempted to make my first stop at the 3-hour mark as this felt like progress and to break the back of the day's cycling (this is probably the wrong analogy in view of my recent injury problems!) My routine for cycles through Wigston is to stop at Costa for what is now standard fuelling of tea to warm up and a treat of millionaire shortbread and a protein bar.

The benefit of cycling similar routes for a large part of the ride is the familiarity and fewer surprises so by now, I have become comfortable with my cycle through the centre of Leicester and the constant stop/start at traffic lights, also the ride on the A6 navigating traffic has become less scary. I left the A6 at Mountsorrel near Loughborough at the 55-mile mark, and although there were only 25 miles left to cycle in the day, the quick turnaround after Reading and the lack of cycling due to my back injury was starting to catch up with me and fatigue started to set in. The final hurdle of the day was as I approached West Bridgford and had to navigate Nottingham rush hour traffic and roadworks which seemed to take an age as the light started to fade. I eventually completed the final 7 miles to Hucknall to finish a long day's cycling – in total, 80 miles and 5 and a half hours of cycling time. My legs were tired and I was looking forward to rest, recovery, food and cider.

During the day, I received an e-mail from Sheffield United, which I only saw in the evening, and they had made an incredible gesture to donate a signed shirt. The responses from the other Championship clubs has been hit and miss but Sheffield United really did support me.

Day 2 to Sheffield United was just over 30 miles and should have been a 2-hour cycle so after a nice breakfast, I set off just after 10 am. The route for the first 12 miles was fairly straightforward through villages adjacent to Mansfield, and it was only just after a village called Skegby that the fun and games commenced. The cycle app was taking me in circles and I reverted to Google maps but the mistake I made was to set the map to walking route and the navigation took me down muddy, uneven tracks. This lasted for about 4 miles, which doesn't sound a lot but seemed like ages. I was now 20 miles from the ground and passed through Bolsover and onto a direct route passing through

Eckington to the outskirts of Sheffield. The last 4 to 5 miles had elevation through traffic but I could see the miles to go reducing and knew I wasn't far away. When I arrived at Sheffield United, the journey had taken 2 and a half hours of cycling time for only 34 miles and over 2 days I had cycled 114 miles in 8 hours, cycling with 5,300 feet elevation. I bike looked like it had been on a rally course.

I was greeted by Stu and Dan with my bag and met Dave who presented me with the signed shirt and I had photos taken in the stadium. After eventually finding the coach, I dropped off the bike and went inside the ground.

Regarding the match, we struggled to get any momentum but were competitive. This was our third game in a week and Sheffield United looked sharper. Having said that, despite the possession and goal attempts, we went into halftime at 0-0. Every Hatters fan would have taken a point from a play-off rival; however, we were not so fortunate as the game turned on a crazy 12 minutes at the start of the second half. We went one behind on 48 minutes and the lead was doubled 3 minutes later, Elijah Adebayo was brought on and we tried to get back in the game which left gaps leaving Reece Burke exposed. He committed a foul and was sent off, which signalled the end of the competition and it was damage limitation from then on – a disappointing result, but on reflection we had taken 6 points from 9 in a week, an incredible win against Bournemouth followed up with a great win at Reading. Nathan Jones had to manage the workload of the squad so rotation of players was inevitable.

This completed January for away games, a brief month for challenges, just Reading and Sheffield United (although I would begin cycling to Swansea for the last few days in January), £532 in donations which just passed the £5,500 mark, a staggering amount at just over halfway. 14 challenges completed with 12 to go. Come on you Hatters!

In terms of games, January would finish with 2 home games. I was lucky enough to be invited by the sponsors thanks to Gary Pettit, and I shared a great evening with Neil, Gill, Yvonne and Nick, who usually sits near me in the kenilworth road stand. To be a guest and experience hospitality for the Bristol City game and even more of a surprise, be presented with the sponsors' signed shirt in recognition of my efforts on my challenge, was totally unexpected and appreciated, something else I never thought would happen when I had planned the challenge many months ago.

# Tuesday 1st February 2022 at 7.45 pm – Swansea City

The Swansea fixture rescheduled from December was arranged for February. Fortunately, this was after the restrictions of attendance in stadiums was lifted. This was going to be one of the hardest rides of the season, which was made more challenging by the strong winds across the 3 days and due to the length of the journey, I was setting off on the Sunday before the Tuesday game, an unusual experience setting off the day after the home 0-0 draw with Blackburn Rovers.

Normally, on multiple days cycling to an away game, I try to do the majority of cycling on the earlier days, leaving a shorter day on match day. However, as it was a midweek game, I didn't want a lot of hanging around wasting time for the game, so this trip was in reverse order. On my first day of the 3-day cycle to Kidlington, I had planned an overnight stay close to Paul, my Bristol City friend. Considering this was the easiest day of the 3, it was harder than I had imagined, partly due to the strong winds, but, I also hadn't realised that due to the weight of my saddle bag, it was dragging on the rear tyre which I didn't realise until I arrived after nearly 3 hours of cycling Ihe impact was that the tyre was completely smooth and had the grip worn away. Anyway, Day 1 was completed – just over 42 miles in nearly 3 hours of cycling, an opportunity to catch up with Paul over a cider and a meal and discuss the recent home win against Bristol City!

After resting, I made a not-too-early start for Day 2. Having checked the tyre was ok and saying my goodbyes to Paul, I took the route through Witney. Now somehow I found myself on the busy A40, where it was even more challenging to navigate traffic on another day of strong winds. It is always a choice between the direct routes on busier but direct roads or the quieter roads that take longer and generally have more elevation and sometimes on uneven road conditions risking potential punctures. I passed through Burford at 17 miles, and through a village called Barnsley. Luckily my navigation wasn't bad enough to end up in the Yorkshire Barnsley! The next checkpoint reached was Cirencester at the 34-mile mark. I had been cycling for 2 and three quarter hours, and the navigation and the strong winds meant I was slightly behind schedule but I also recognised that I needed to take on nutrition and carbohydrate fuelling.

Although it stayed dry, the winds made the temperatures fresh with 5 degrees feeling like zero. My usual strategy when I am feeling tired and cold is to focus on 5-mile markers and I crossed off the miles – approaching 50 miles is always a landmark. Wotton-under-Edge was a checkpoint at the 57-mile mark and was the point where the elevation would ease up. I had only -20 more miles to do that day but I still had to navigate the Severn Bridge. 9 miles later, I reached Thornbury, but not before navigation took me up muddy country lanes with no grip on the rear tyre, all part of the adventure. In Thornbury, I stopped at a cake shop – anyone who knows my routine by now will know it consists of millionaire shortbread (my treat), tea and a protein bar for recovery.

It was a reasonably short ride to the Severn Bridge, while praying they hadn't done the unthinkable and closed it to cyclists. Luckily, they hadn't and a short distance across the bridge, I reached Chepstow and my accommodation for the night. Day 2 completed, a hard 77 miles in 5 and a half hours of cycling with challenging 4,000 feet elevation. I had very tired legs, and a bonus was that the room had a bath to help them recover. Now this was also transfer deadline day so after food and drink I stayed up for news of pending transfers, which didn't happen. I wasn't too disappointed; we had a great squad for the remaining games and I would see where it took us!

Day 3 was going to be another tough day's cycling but I made it into Wales and the last day until I got to watch my beloved Luton Town. I started without breakfast, hoping to pass a McDonald's, a calculated risk but it paid off just before Newport at the 17-mile mark. It was a challenge to navigate my way around the Newport Docks, avoid joining the M4 and attempt to make my way towards Caerphilly. Now the navigation took me off the direct busier roads through a number of villages, which would usually be fine but this route took me up a few difficult climbs, at which point I had only cycled 25 miles and still had another 50 miles to go to reach the stadium. I took the decision that I would take the busier main roads where it was safe to avoid further fatigue on my legs, a different kind of motivation when the roads look the same. I was just trying to cross off the mileage interval targets, and there were still strong winds so I just had to push on.

Another motivation to get there was that Stu had messaged and asked if I wanted to commentate with Simon Pitts. Now, I had thought that this opportunity had passed after the cancellation of the game in December, so it was a privilege that I didn't want to pass up, and I happily accepted with feelings of nerves and excitement, although I didn't have time to think about it much while navigating my way through Wales.

I was crossing off the checkpoints en route and reached the region of Bridgend at 48 miles, which had taken 4 and a half hours of cycling and I still had nearly 30 miles to go. I could hear my legs complaining! The next checkpoint would be Port Talbot, about 15 miles away, just over an hour of cycling. I didn't think much beyond this point, as the wind picked up again, the roads were getting busier and my legs more tired. I reached this checkpoint after 6 hours of cycling time.

Only 11 miles to go, the end was in sight or so I thought, as I headed along Swansea Bay to make the turn into Swansea. Now up to that point I had been taking the direct busy roads, but when you are tired and fatigued, the brain stops functioning too, but on this occasion I realised the direct road would take me into Swansea Docks not anywhere near the ground. The cycle app appeared to take me on the M4 but after some thinking time there was a cycle path that took me alongside the M4. The final challenge was not concentrating on the cycle path and ending up on a muddy path entering a field. The final time to engage brain and get back on track, the ride that I thought would never end eventually did after 74 miles, 5 and a half hours of cycling time, with over 7 hours since I had left Chepstow. In total, my 3 days cycling to Swansea had taken 193 miles, 14 hours' cycling time not including breaks, and more than 8,000 feet of elevation climbs. I was exhausted but happy to arrive.

I was welcomed by Stu and Dan and had the usual photos taken in front of the Swansea sign. At this point, I had no idea how incredible the evening would turn out to be. Stu had arranged for me to have a media pass and after I had changed, I joined Stu, Dan, Simon and the team for a curry while waiting for the game to start. I dropped my bike off on the Bobbers Travel coach, then the nerves started to kick in for my co-commentary with Simon. I had no need to be nervous, Simon was brilliant, he made me feel so relaxed and involved me in the commentary at the right moments. It's experiences like this when you appreciate what a professional Simon is and how easy he makes it look.

Another incredible moment was an announcement over the loudspeaker before the game mentioning my ride. The response from all the fans was unbelievable and an emotional experience.

The game was perfect on so many levels, and it was an unreal experience to co-commentate with Simon Pitts. I remember asking how I should react if we scored, to which Simon replied, 'Like a fan'. The game commenced and we started positively looking dangerous moving forward, especially James Bree causing problems down the wing. Although we had the better chances, Swansea grew into the game and although they had the majority of possession, they didn't carry any real threat. The second half continued with the same pattern then Nathan made a double substitution, bringing on Cameron Jerome and Harry Cornick and they combined perfectly for Harry to convert a great opportunity with a great finish and I could celebrate on the commentary with a yell along the lines of 'Get in there, Harry Cornick!'. Although Swansea pressed, we looked solid and held on for a professional away win, cue the celebrations, Harry doing a cycle celebration dance and Nathan climbing the barrier in the Luton End to celebrate. Come on you Hatters! What a win!

My surprises hadn't finished as Stu asked me to stay behind for some photos. Unknown to me, Harry surprised me by coming into the stand to give me his shirt and he shared some generous, kind words about my rides. Also, I wasn't aware until a few days later that Harry had recorded a message endorsing my ride and asking people to donate, an incredible gesture. I was buzzing to get the shirt, I had wanted one all season but felt it inappropriate to ask. As if that wasn't enough, Stu said that Nathan wanted to chat and while I waited for Nathan to finish his media commitments, I had a nice chat with Mick Harford, a genuine nice guy and an absolute Luton Town legend. Nathan was also complimentary about my epic ride to Swansea and we chatted about the game for a bit before I made my way back to the coach where I was greeted by loud applause!

The journey home was long (but not 3 days!) and I eventually got back to Flitwick about 3.15 am, ready for my final 45-minute journey home. I didn't sleep too much on the coach, mainly due to excitement, and on the final cycle home it was surprisingly mild considering the time and I eventually reached home just after 4 am, needing time to unwind so it was 5 am before I got 3 hours' sleep before starting work, very tired but extremely happy. Swansea had been the most exhausting challenge and the most amazing experience.

Also, the Swansea challenge had an unbelievable impact on donations – the brilliant endorsements from the club and the exposure that my 3-day ride had created, had resulted in nearly £2,000 being raised across 10 days from when I set off for Swansea, which was 23% of all donations over the 6 months. Everyone's generosity and kind words of encouragement left me speechless and feeling emotional. The total raised had nearly reached a staggering £7,500.

# Saturday 5th February 2022 at 5.30 pm – Cambridge United FA Cup 4th Round

I had 3 days to recover from my long cycle to Swansea, and fortunately, with the next game being the FA Cup, the gods were smiling on me, giving me an away tie to raise more awareness and donations whilst giving me one of the least demanding rides to Cambridge and even a 5.30 pm kickoff, so I could get a lie-in.

I set off just after 11 am. There were several routes that I could take but I headed out towards Bedford, through Kempston, en route to Sandy. On arrival near Sandy it dawned on me as I cycled through a village called Moggerhanger that an easier route which was also a regular training ride was available that would have avoided Kempston/Bedford traffic, but it made the ride interesting! At this point, I had reached the halfway point at 26 miles, although it was windy which seemed to have been a common theme on my recent rides. Riding through Cambridgeshire, I had the benefit of cycling with little or no elevation so it wasn't too tiring on the legs at this stage. It always seems like I make progress as I cycle through the counties so knowing that I had entered Cambridgeshire felt like I was making progress while passing through a number of villages on quiet roads with a low volume of traffic. This was until I reached near Cambourne at the 41-mile mark.

The last 10 miles were on the busier direct roads into Cambridge but it was an uneventful ride without any dramas despite the busy traffic and I arrived at 3pm to complete Away Cycle Challenge 16, cycling 51 miles in just under 3 hours and 15 minutes with only 1,300 feet elevation. This was probably only second to Stevenage for the least challenging of my rides.

I always enjoyed going to Cambridge United, but in the years of our rise through the leagues, we hadn't played there for a while – probably one of the most memorable games was the draw in the 13/14 season that virtually guaranteed our promotion as champions from the Conference.

In the days leading up to the game, I received positive support from Cambridge United, who kindly arranged for me to have photos taken inside the ground before the game and I met Dave, an official from Cambridge United FC who took me inside the ground and took some photos. I also met Gareth Owen, Luton's official photographer, who also took photos and to my surprise, the photo was used by the club in a great Twitter post along the lines of 'We have arrived and look who else is here' – brilliant exposure before the game.

On route to a nearby McDonald's for a pre-match recovery meal, I bumped into some supporters of both teams, who had been following my progress. It is so nice to get to meet so many amazing people and at the time, I have no idea who they are until they introduce themselves but it's great to put a face to the Twitter names and their support. So, after feeding myself I got a call from Les from the Bobbers Travel Club to say the coach was waiting outside the ground to take my bike before it moved on to be parked. Everyone connected with the Bobbers is so helpful. After loading my bike on the coach and changing, I made my way into the ground, walking across a cattle grid and a field to get to the stand. I definitely don't get this experience in the Championship.

I felt quietly confident but wary of a Cup upset, especially with the number of changes Nathan Jones had made, giving a debut to Elliot Thorpe and rare starts to Carlos Mendes Gomes and Admiral Muskwe. The first 10 minutes were nervy with a cup-tie atmosphere but when we opened the scoring from a Reece Burke header we settled down to dominate the game and the gulf in quality was evident at the half-hour mark as we went 2-0 ahead with a great finish from Carlos Mendes Gomes. We got to halftime 2-0 ahead, knowing if we were professional we would see the game out without any dramas. It was an uneventful second half, as Cambridge couldn't threaten us, and we scored a third goal in the final minute in front of the Luton fans, courtesy of a Muskwe goal to complete a convincing win and then across the cattle grids back on the coach, very happy for the short journey back to Flitwick via Luton.

Up until the journey home with a win secured, I didn't want to look too far ahead to the 5$^{th}$ round, as the draw would have an impact on my challenge as it was being played 3 days before Middlesbrough away and would mean leaving the day after the 5<sup>th</sup> round. Anyway, we drew with Chelsea at home, a great draw to challenge ourselves against the European champions even though I was hoping for another away trip.

So, the coach arrived at Flitwick about 9.45 pm and I cycled my final cycle home of the day. which took nearly an hour due to forgetting my front light bracket and having to balance the front light in front of me while cycling home. Anyway, I got home just after 10.30 pm, another great day completing another challenge and watching a good away win by the Hatters. Come on you Hatters!

# Saturday 12th February 2022 at 3 pm – Birmingham City

I had the benefit of a week's rest and recovery from the Cambridge ride, which hadn't been too demanding, so it was a good week to prepare for Birmingham, including a home win against Barnsley – not convincing but it was 3 points and I travelled to Birmingham City in a positive frame of mind.

The Birmingham City ride would be an early start – usually, for a Saturday 3 pm kick-off, I try not to leave myself more than 40/50 miles to get there for around 1 pm in case of any navigation or mechanical issues, so this challenge was going to be just over 75 miles. Being a northern ride, I didn't want to drop the car off in Newport Pagnell on the morning, so I made the drop-off on the Friday morning before work and an extended 16-mile cycle home was my final preparation.

I set off from home at 7.13 am and took a different route from the West Bromwich Albion challenge, heading through North Milton Keynes out to Stony Stratford, then to Deanshanger. My next check point was Whittlebury, with no need to follow my navigation as it was signposted, or so I thought – either I missed a sign or it was wrongly signposted, obviously the first one! After eventually finding Whittlebury, I cycled through Silverstone at the 23-mile mark. It was another fresh ride, officially 4 degrees but it felt much colder. I had decided to wear my thermal gloves but settled for 2 pairs of socks instead of warmer overshoes, as cold feet aren't as big of an issue as cold hands, but the nature of the feet position clipped into the cleats mean it's difficult to get warm. Anyway, I progressed on my route, checking off the villages: Blakesley, then Preston Capes, Napton on the Hill, which won't mean anything to anyone but it meant I was making slow progress. At this point I had cycled 42 miles and this was just over halfway.

It's normally at this point, when I have been cycling approaching the 3-hour mark, that I look to find a café or coffee shop for a break. Unfortunately, this route was all on quieter roads through villages and I didn't find anything and as I reached Stoneleigh at 54 miles, I could see on my navigation map that I was south of Coventry so my estimate was that I couldn't be more than 20-25 miles away, so even if I found somewhere, I might as well push on and get to the ground and hopefully get out of the cold.

The next major checkpoint was entering the Solihull area and some of the route became familiar from my West Bromwich cycle, even though it was 6 months previously and I had only made the cycle on one occasion, so my memory was surprising! At this point, I had nearly cycled 70 miles and had only between 5 and 10 miles to go, which was encouraging news, although I was expecting to encounter some busy traffic. It was a clue that I was on the right track when I found myself on Birmingham Road and when I saw signs to Acocks Green, Small Heath and Bordesley Green, I knew that I was in the suburbs of Birmingham and I wasn't too far away.

So, eventually I arrived at Birmingham City just after 1 pm after cycling 78 miles. It had taken 5 hours 13 minutes of cycling. Away Cycle Challenge 17 was completed, only 8 more to go unless we made the playoffs! The elevation had been just over 3,500 feet, but it didn't feel like it, as there weren't any seriously difficult climbs, just a lot of inclines (not hills!) which allowed me to progress at a steady pace while battling the winds – which again was becoming a common theme.

After arriving at Birmingham City I tried to find the players' entrance to wish the team good luck and catch Stu or Dan to get my bag. I was directed by a steward, not knowing the teams had a different entrance and was sent to the Birmingham City players' entrance. I bumped into a local supporter, Linzi, who was very friendly and complimentary about my ride, and asked me for a photo (a new experience) and directed me to the away entrance, which is different to some grounds where you can't just follow the stadium. I had to navigate through streets to an entrance out the back, the team coach arrived and I had a nice chat with the birthday boy and Luton legend Mick Harford, an incredible guy, who offered his continued support for my challenge. Now I was still in all my cycling gear with my bike and I got an interesting reaction from Pelly and Kal Naismith, asking me if I was still cycling! So, after a fist pump from Harry Cornick, I made my way round the ground to have my usual photo taken by Gaz, always a friendly face when I arrive, and a brief chat with Gary Sweet, then made my way to the coach

As I mentioned before, everyone was in a positive mood. Surely, we were going to put right the 0-5 hammering Birmingham City gave us in the home fixture? How wrong we were. After a positive opening with 10 minutes of dominating, we thought it only a matter of time before we scored, then came the tennis balls on the pitch protesting about their owners, stewards on the pitch while the game continued and against the run of play they scored around the half-hour mark. We never troubled them again, especially after conceding in the first 30 seconds of the second half to a player we love to hate, Lyle Taylor. We always give him stick and he, more often than not, seems to score, which he did to make it 2-0 and end the contest. To make it worse, it ended 3-0 – incredibly, that was an aggregate score of 0-8, if ever a song of 'Can we play you every week' was needed, this was the game and opponent it was made for.

So, back on the coach for the journey home, where everyone had a vote for Man of the Match. Across both coaches there were 34 'no' votes, which sums the game up, although looking at the overall season, we must have been massively happy and impressed. Come on you Hatters!

The coach made good progress despite the Birmingham traffic, and I was back at my car for just after 7 pm, and with time for a cup of tea and a chat with David and Barbara, who kindly look after my car for the northern trips, which saves me a further cycle home, unlike the southern cycling home from Flitwick. Time to rest up and recover.

# Wednesday 23rd February 2022 at 8 pm – Stoke City

I was back on 2 wheels for Away Cycle Challenge 18 to Stoke City. The distance was just over 110 miles, which was a long day's cycling for one day but too short to split over 2 days and also, I didn't have the luxury of being able to take a day's leave. Anyway, I approached the day's cycling in a nervous mood as it had been 4 months since I had completed a 6/7 hour cycle, with Preston being the last one.

So, I set off just after 9 am on my familiar route towards Northampton. I had allowed enough time to take stops; however, not long into the ride I encountered road closures near Salcey Forest, and although I was initially allowed through, a few miles later I was turned back and had to to take a detour which added 7 miles to the ride. I passed through Northampton at 22 miles on my familiar route towards Lutterworth – normally I arrive there at 36/37 miles and less than 3 hours but I had the extra miles from the diversion.

Rather than stop at Lutterworth, I decided to progress further before stopping at a place called Stoney Stanton, which was at the 54-mile mark and there I stopped at a café I had used before. Normally, it's a brief stop for cake and tea but on this occasion, I felt that I needed a longer stop to get warm, as it was another ride in cold conditions. I treated myself to soup, a roll, tea and cake, more than I am used to taking on mid-ride and I felt it as I started off again, a lesson learned for future rides – stick to the usual recovery and comfort foods for a mid-ride break.

The next 20 odd miles were mainly uneventful as I reached Burton upon Trent at the 75-mile mark. I was able to tick off the checkpoints through various villages en route and although tired, I had predicted that I had about 35 miles to go, which would be just over 2 hours of cycling plus any traffic to navigate. I avoided the temptation to stop again to arrive before it got dark and around Sudbury I encountered more road closure signs. As I mentioned previously, most of them don't stop me cycling through and this was the case, although some navigating of the bike on grassy, muddy verges to avoid workmen and their trucks was necessary, while always being polite to avoid being told to turn around.

Between Sudbury and Uttoxeter, the elevation started to increase for the last 25 miles, just as my legs started to complain! It shouldn't be a surprise, having done this route for a number of trips, that I reverted to focusing on the next 5-mile strategy, which usually helps. My next challenge was that my devices started to warn of low battery, most importantly of which was my phone, which was operating my navigation, and secondly, my Garmin, which went to battery-saving mode and thirdly, my watch, which was my back-up for data. Normally, I could stop for a recharge blast but the light was fading so I had added motivation to complete the final 10 miles through traffic.

So, Away Cycle Challenge 18 was finally completed, cycling 111 miles with just under 7 and a half hours of cycling time and just over 5,000 feet elevation – a tough day's cycling but another challenge achieved.

As the light had faded, I made my way to the ground reception in the hope I could get some photos inside, and initially, I wasn't sure if I would be successful but then a number of staff who were aware of my efforts through my prior communication came to meet me and let me inside the ground to get some photos – a great welcome from another Championship club. After the photos, I found the coach and got changed and took my seat for the game.

Regarding the game, Stoke City were another of our bogey teams that we hadn't beaten in a long while, so we entered the ground in hope rather than expectation, but the team did us all proud. It was a nervy first half, although there were a few chances and it was 0-0 at half time. The team improved dramatically in the second half, kicking towards the Luton fans. The movement and passing were quicker and we went into wild celebrations 11 minutes into the second half when we scored with a trademark super Danny Hylton striker's goal, finding space from close distance to finish and when Cameron Jerome added a second with 10 minutes to go we felt the win was a formality until we switched off in the last minute to concede and then saw 7 minutes' injury time go up. A nervous finish but we held on for a great, rare win against Stoke City and a happy coach journey home and after collecting my car, I eventually got home tired but happy and buzzing. Come on you Hatters!

# Saturday 5th March at 3 pm – Middlesbrough

Following the Stoke City trip, I had a week's recovery and preparation for Away Cycle Challenge 19 to Middlesbrough, so I had a few indoor sessions and a Sunday 40-mile ride to tick over – nice and steady rides, low intensity just to keep my legs working, saving energy and preparing for the hardest challenge of the season.

The day before leaving for Middlesbrough was consumed with a home game against Chelsea in the FA Cup. After dropping off the car in Newport Pagnell with a 10-mile ride home in the rain, the Chelsea game was a great opportunity in front of the cameras to test ourselves against the world champions. Not surprisingly, players were rested for Middlesbrough and we gave a good account, losing 3-2 despite leading twice. I'm never happy to lose a game but I felt very proud of how far we had come to compete against Chelsea's million-pound stars!

Arriving home after the game, I did the final preparation for my gruelling 3-day trip to Middlesbrough, which would be around 240 miles. Unlike other challenges, there wasn't an easier day ahead and mentally I prepared for a tough challenge that would test me both physically and mentally. I got about 4 hours' sleep the night before, not ideal but it was hard to switch off after the Chelsea game.

The route on Day 1 was to Newark-on-Trent, approximately 100 miles, and it took me on a different route that I hadn't taken before. Up to now, the north-west/midlands rides had started with familiar routes, so it was nice to see a different route but this focused my mind on avoiding getting lost. I headed out near Olney and took the A509 to Wellingborough, a road I knew well but not on a bike. From there I took the back roads to Rothwell, where I stopped for my first break, finding a coffee shop at 44 miles. I spoke to Les from Bobbers Travel, who was updating me on the M1 closures for the way home, so potentially, I might have a Flitwick cycle home but that wasn't a concern at this point! I was almost halfway for the day, and the weather conditions were dry, sunny and fresh without being brutally cold.

The second half of Day 1 was spent navigating my way through Leicestershire and touching Lincolnshire borders. From about the 55-mile point for 20-25 miles the elevation was a bit lumpy (cycling saying for up/down elevation) – steady, not brutal. I passed through Melton Mowbray at the 74-mile mark, and I was now three-quarters of the way to completing Day 1. As I approached the last 5-10 miles and the usual country roads the cycle nav wanted to take me on, but instead it took me on a narrow road with gates. Who puts a bloody gate halfway up a hill?! But it gave me the opportunity to chat to a local for a while and subsequently I found a donation days later. I really do get to meet some lovely people on my challenge.

So, eventually, Day 1 was completed, and I reached my Day 1 Airbnb accommodation after 100 miles – just over 6 and a half hours moving time and 8 and a half hours since leaving home, with 5,000 feet elevation. My legs were tired and needing a rest and recovery. It was my first time in Newark-on-Trent and I found a nice pub to get fed. The accommodation was just what I needed, I have never had a bad experience with Airbnb and Tanya was lovely and helpful.

Day 2 of Away Cycle Challenge 19 was due to have similar distances to Day 1, but the elevation was to be less demanding, at a third of the previous day. However, the weather would be a leveller. I was awake early to not only prepare for the day ahead but to do a Radio Tees interview at 7.50 am. The radio station had been supportive of my challenge, interviewing me the day before I set off and they wanted to chat to me for an update after Day 1. The exposure was a great help for raising awareness. Rain started to fall early in the morning and continued as I set off from Newark-on-Trent just before 8.30 am for Day 2. Although the forecast for most of the day was light rain, I hoped it wouldn't follow me all day.

From Newark-on-Trent, I headed on my way through the various towns/villages in Nottinghamshire. In the distance were the power stations, which it seemed I never left behind, and it appeared to took forever to leave the county of Nottinghamshire.

There was no let-up in the rain and with the temperatures not rising above 37 degrees F, it was going to be a long, cold day. I passed through Gainsborough at the 28-mile mark and although ready to stop, I wanted to pass the halfway mark before stopping, as this helps with my mental preparation for coping with the day. Eventually, I stopped in a town called Thorne at 50 miles and found a coffee shop. The stop was for 45 minutes, longer than usual, but I wanted to get warm and dry off.

I had about 40 miles left to complete the day and my checkpoints ahead were Selby and York. The route to Selby was straightforward and I followed my navigation app. The route to York took me on the busy A19, despite efforts to find quieter roads but also, by this stage, I was cold and tired and just wanted to get to my destination. I navigated through the York traffic to a place called Tollerton where I was staying. I had finally completed Day 2 with 93 miles cycled with a moving time of 6 and a half hours and a total of 8 hours, with at least 6 of these out in the rain.

The farmhouse where I was staying wasn't the warmest, not what I needed after a long, cold day, but I found a pub opposite with a fire, good food and drink – just what I needed!

The final day of Away Cycle Challenge 19 was the shortest in distance but would be the most challenging due to the climbs across the North Yorkshire moors, but at least the day started dry and the sunshine made an appearance.

I eased into Day 3 as I cycled to Easingwold and the tough climbs started around 15 miles and it would be another 20 miles before my climbing for the day would be finished. I missed a turning, but the navigation app recalculated, and unknown to me at the time, it was a muddy path due to the weather and my tyres couldn't grip going up hills. Also, with the mud in my cleats, I couldn't clip the shoes in and get any leverage to get power to climb the hills so eventually I admitted defeat and went back to the original route up to the top. By this stage all the climbs were a struggle and the previous 2 days were taking their toll on my legs, but I pushed on. Even the descents were challenging due to the amount of water that had fallen in recent days.

The saying about laws of gravity applies to cycle climbs and I knew that eventually I would reach the top but before I did, I found a shop with a tearoom, because my Day 2 accommodation was in a quiet location without breakfast facilities. I had started without breakfast so my stop at about 30 miles was after just over 3 hours' cycling, so a brief stop for tea and scones was much needed.

I paid particular focus to my map on my navigation, as moving away from the dark green bits into the lighter green areas meant the worst of the climbs were coming to an end around the 35-mile mark. The navigation was directing me to a village called Ingleby Greenhow, but I had also seen signs on busy A roads to Middlesbrough. I just wanted to get the challenge completed as soon as possible so I took this route, which was 14 miles long, and I was on countdown to reach my destination.

Eventually, I reached the riverside stadium. Day 3 was only 49 miles but had taken me 4 hours with 3,500 feet elevation. Over the 3 days, I had cycled 240 miles, cycling for 17 hours with 10,000 feet elevation, but finally Away Cycle Challenge 19 had been achieved, the toughest challenge so far.

Just as I arrived, it started to hail. I was greeted by Middlesbrough's supporter liaison officer, who wasn't aware of my challenge but seemed a bit embarrassed that I had previously emailed but it hadn't been read! Anyway, I managed to get a few photos outside the ground and found the Bobbers Travel Club to offload my bike and messaged Stu and Dan to get my bag of warm clothes to change into.

Fortunately, Stu managed to get me access into the media room and I was fed with shepherd's pie, perfect after a day without proper food. Even better, I was allowed into the ground to have photos taken in the dugout by the official photographers and also on my phone. Dan did a brilliant post on the Luton Town Twitter page to help with awareness of my challenge and after this I made my way back to the coach to change.

I entered the ground hoping to see a great away win to make my trip worthwhile, but unfortunately, it was a long journey to see a disappointing defeat. We were all full of optimism, especially as key players were rested from the Chelsea game. We did create opportunities in the first half through Cameron Jerome and Elijah Adebayo, but they didn't materialize and we were punished by a harsh penalty after quarter of an hour. Even more disappointing was to pick up more injuries to Kal Naismith and Gabriel Osho, and afterwards Middlesbrough doubled their lead. Although Harry pulled a goal back it was only a consolation, so then it was back on the coach for the long journey home.

So, because of the M1 being closed at Northampton, the coach took the direct route back to Luton, and as a result, I had to get off the coach at Flitwick, as I would normally do for a southern game. Therefore, my cycling wasn't finished for the day so at 10.30 pm, I started my 50-minute and 11-mile cycle home to complete an exhausting trip to Middlesbrough. To think I wanted to draw with Middlesbrough away in the Cup, what was I thinking? Once is enough, although we could be playing them again in the playoffs. Come on you Hatters!

MIDDLESBROUGH FC
RIVERSIDE STADIUM
MIDDLESBROUGH AFC
ryebridge

# Tuesday 8th March at 7.45 pm – Coventry City

It was another quick turnaround after the gruelling 3-day trip to Middlesbrough with just 2 days until I set off for Away Cycle Challenge 20 to Coventry City. A complete rest day had been followed by a 45-minute easy, high-cadence recovery session. Luckily, I wasn't expecting a demanding ride and gave myself enough time to take it at a steady pace. I had worked in the morning, everything was packed the night before and I set off just after 1 pm. The temperature was 10 celsius degrees and with some sunshine it didn't feel cold, so it was a pleasant ride. The route took me through Milton Keynes and my usual backroads to Northampton, passing the Sixfields Stadium, then to Duston.

At this point I had reached the 25-mile mark and it took me a while to get my bearings as I took a different route from the other routes that headed towards Leicester. The route was straightforward as I headed towards Daventry. After a few wrong turnings, I headed on the quieter village roads towards Rugby, which took me up to the 45-mile mark. I had been cycling for about 3 hours and by my calculation, I had about 15 miles to go and one hour's cycling left.

My route was planned with the intention of avoiding cycling through the centre of Coventry as I headed towards Binley, which is on the outskirts of Coventry, and about 5 miles away. Even though I was avoiding the centre, I was hitting rush hour traffic and battling the constant traffic lights stopping me on red and navigating the impatient traffic which didn't want to give way for cyclists. The final mile towards the ground was on a busy dual carriageway that led to the approach to the Coventry Building Society Arena (I always remember it as the Ricoh Arena). I could see the ground on my right but getting off the dual carriageway caused its own challenges, but I eventually arrived.

I had completed Away Cycle Challenge 20, cycling 60 miles, which had taken me 4 hours with a not-too-demanding 2,400 feet of elevation.

I hung around the players' entrance and met some supporters of both teams who were interested to know about my challenge and a few Coventry supporters wanted to donate. As I have mentioned before, throughout my challenge, I have got to meet some brilliant people. I feel very fortunate and it was a benefit I hadn't expected when I started out in August. It is also nice to get to meet the officials from the opposing teams who I contact through emails, who are all so supportive despite me having no affiliation to the home team. The wider football community really do come together for great causes.

Not long after, the Bobbers Travel coaches arrived and I was able to offload my bike and get changed for the game. It seems that it is becoming more of a rush to get into the ground on time for the game, which is a positive as I get great positive feedback outside the ground and not because I get lost en route.

In the build-up to this challenge, I had been messaging Dave from 'Oh when the town' podcast and we were to meet to discuss Luke joining me on the Peterborough ride. I managed to catch up with the guys at the bar inside the ground. Their podcast had been a great comfort to me during the lockdown, when I had been really struggling with my mental health and it was great to chat with them and sit with them for the game.

There was a great turnout by Hatters fans, just over 1,700 for a mid-week game. We weren't at our best during the first half, conceding possession, but Coventry wasn't creating many chances. Then, at 38 minutes, a moment of quality – a long kick by Alex Palmer, not cleared, which found its way through to Elijah Adebayo for a clinical finish. A rare moment of quality ending the first half at 1-0 up, it shows that having that quality at this level makes all the difference. After retiring to the bar at halftime for a drink, the second half was best summed up as a professional away performance holding on to the win. We rarely looked in trouble, although Coventry's best chance came with 10 minutes to go, missing a point-blank opportunity, a heart-in-mouth moment, but we had ground out a clinical 1-0 win away from home, thanks to a great save from Palmer, keeping a clean sheet in what turned out to be the final appearance of his emergency loan.

So back on the coach and a happy journey home after our impressive form. Fortunately, the M1 stayed open so I could collect my car in Newport Pagnell and get home at a reasonable time and reflect on another away cycle challenge completed, backed up with another impressive win. All was good, although this was about to change a few days later.

# COVID-19 and postponed Hull City away cycle challenge - 19th March

The day following the Coventry City game I took a COVID-19 test (my usual routine) which was negative and was looking forward to the QPR game on Sunday. My plans changed the day before as I woke up feeling completely drained with no energy and unusually for someone that functions on 5 hours' sleep a night, I slept all day Saturday and most of the evening. I presumed this was just a cold so wasn't too concerned. My new batch of COVID-19 test kits arrived, so as a precaution I took a test on Sunday morning. Getting ready for the QPR game whilst I waited for the result, I was gutted to see it come back positive, so I had to watch the QPR game at home. I wasn't in the best of moods, which became a lot worse after the game. Why can't we ever beat QPR? We played ok but basic errors cost us.

As I continued with my isolation over the next few days, I was hoping over the next week that I would get the negative test to get back to normality. I had written off the Preston game, which was Day 5 since the symptoms had started, and I watched an impressive 4-0 home win on TV which cheered me up. I was starting to improve, although it was difficult to monitor from sitting doing nothing!

I still tested positive the day after the Preston game (Day 6) and at this point I was starting to stress about the upcoming Hull City away cycle challenge 2 days away. I was in regular contact with Stewart from the Bobbers Travel Club and spoke on the Bobbers Travel live show that evening, still hoping to make the trip. Those that know me, will know how determined I am and having made the commitment to cycle to every away game, failing wasn't an option- I just needed a negative test and I would set off on the 2-day cycle – this really was so important to me, to keep the awareness and donations going, but I also had to take the emotion out of the decision and do what was best for my health and respectful of people I would come into contact with.

The day before the Hull City game and the day I was due to leave, I was up at 4 am, packing to set off in preparation for another COVID-

19 test. I remember having taken the test about 5.30 am, after which I was pacing around the house, building myself up to check the result. It was positive. I was devastated and in tears. I couldn't make the Hull City trip and informed Stewart. Now, I knew that everyone would understand, and no one would criticise me for not making the trip – even so, it didn't make me feel any better.

On the day of the game, I shared the news on social media, and received so many good wishes and messages, especially from the club – even though the media team were at the stadium preparing for the game, they still found time to put out a tweet asking people to donate and send me good wishes, an amazing gesture which cheered me up, even more so to see such an impressive win with a dominant performance, including a wonderful free kick from James Bree.

I next tested on Monday 21st March, with a negative result, and followed this up with a second consecutive negative test the day after. I was finally COVID-free 9 days from a positive to negative test. Despite being upset at missing the Hull City challenge, on reflection, I put it into perspective and a lot of people have had it a lot worse, and I should be grateful that I have made a full recovery.

# Saturday 26th and Sunday 27th March – Hull City

I know that no one expected me to complete the Hull City challenge, having missed the game with COVID-19 but for me it was never an option not to complete the challenge even though there was no game when I arrived. I thought of the charities and all the selfless work they do and all the people that struggle and need the charities' support, who must keep going and giving up isn't an option and it wasn't for me.

The weekend following the Hull City game was a free weekend, though there were international games so really it was the only opportunity to cycle to Hull, so I made the necessary preparations. The biggest challenge was how I was going to get home, which wasn't helped by a Pennine train strike so trains couldn't get me home without multiple changes with a bike. I knew before that this challenge without the Bobbers Travel support would be almost impossible, and I realised this even more after this weekend.

My only option without using more holiday and extra hotel costs was to use my contacts through work to get a logistics company to drive my car up north for my drive home at a reasonable cost of £70. Now they advised the driver would take it to his house in Scunthorpe, not too far to cycle to from Hull, until I found out he actually lived near Scunthorpe the other side of the River Trent with a detour to get across the river. Anyway, on the Friday, I dropped off my car, and had a 10-mile cycle home to prepare for setting off for Hull.

On the Saturday, I had a prior engagement between 11 am and midday so I had a break after 7 miles. I was greeted by lovely sunshine in the morning, a strange experience to cycle wearing shorts, fingerless gloves and without multiple thermal layers.

So, I set off after my engagement just before midday and my Day 1 route would take me just over 80 miles and on a different route that I hadn't been on before. The unknown factor was if I had fully recovered from COVID-19 – in the previous 2 weeks since testing positive, I had just done a few indoor sessions of about an hour and I was going to embark on a 6-hour ride. I was living up to my Mad Hatter Mark name!

I cycled through Olney and into Northamptonshire, passing through Rushden, Irchester and Irthlingborough, heading towards the Cambridgeshire border. I cycled through Oundle at the 43-mile mark and needed a rest to recover, as the sunshine (not that I was complaining) and lack of training meant my legs were starting to feel tired so I fed myself on a sausage roll, carrot cake and drink. This was also an opportunity to recharge all my devices. I was about halfway so I felt I was making progress.

As I cycled through Cambridgeshire into Lincolnshire, it was a sign that I was nearing the end but I was starting to fatigue. Stamford was reached at 58 miles, which was a familiar area as my dad had previously lived near here so the journey to Bourne was straightforward at the 68-mile mark. As my legs were tiring more as each mile passed, I took the most direct route on the A15 for the final 17 miles, and although the elevation wasn't too demanding, the wind had picked up and it was a struggle mentally, so I adopted my usual strategy of focussing on 5-mile segments. Eventually, I arrived, having completed Day 1 of Away Cycle Challenge 21 of 86 miles in just under 6 hours of cycling time. I was shattered and didn't feel great – not just the fatigue but the effects of COVID-19 had caught up with me. Knowing how I was feeling, I was nervous about Day 2, even though it would only be 65 miles plus getting back to my car. I booked an Airbnb in Sleaford, and the couple were lovely and so accommodating, even driving me into town to get fed. I didn't stay long before resting and recovering before Day 2.

I prepared for Day 2, rested and made a final check for the route and my journey from Hull and found a route that would mean a shorter cycle after arriving in Hull, a relief as I wanted to reduce cycling time where possible. I set off just before 9.30 am.

For the first 20 miles, in proximity to Lincoln, I felt really good considering how I had felt the night before and I cycled at a steady pace. The route took me through a number of small towns/villages and was largely uneventful as I crossed off the checkpoints. I didn't see any cafés so I progressed towards Brigg, which would be a significant landmark of 47 miles and would start the 20-mile countdown. The early morning energy had now disappeared and the chill was replaced by warmer temperatures and sunshine, t-shirt and shorts weather. I reached Brigg after 3 and a half hours and 47 miles, and the next major checkpoint was Barton-upon-Humber, then the Humber Bridge. Normally, when I see the end in sight, I revert to the fastest route on busy main roads but on this occasion, I kept to the shorter route, a wise decision to avoid the A15. I eventually crossed the Humber Bridge at 60 miles into Hessle as I entered Hull, and from my time in Hull visiting relatives, I knew I wasn't far away, having seen their unique cream-coloured phone boxes!

I finally arrived at the MKM stadium, completing the 66 miles in just under 4 and a half hours – in total, Away Cycle Challenge 21 had taken just under 11 hours of cycling and 152 miles with 5,000 feet elevation. Although the ground was locked up, I found some local park grounds people to take my usual arrival photos. It was a strange experience to not be greeted by fans and a lot of activity, an anti-climax in some ways, but I had achieved what I'd set out to do.

Now the additional challenge of getting home commenced. Arriving at around 3 pm, I contacted the driver to find out the keys weren't there for him to take my car. In a state of panic, I cycled to the train station, where I would take the 30-minute train to Goole. By this point, the keys were found and the driver was on his way, expecting to arrive at 6 pm, so I decided to pass a few hours in Wetherspoons with a meal and a cider before setting off for my final cycle of the challenge, 11 miles to where my car would be. With my bike loaded in the car, I started my 3-hour drive home just before 7 pm, eventually getting home just before 10.30 pm – time to rest and recover from a challenging 2 days.

This was my final challenge of March and had raised an additional £605 this month, taking the total donations to £8,950, just short of £9K, an unbelievable amount and £1,000 short of the £10K target I thought would be an impossible dream. Just like the brilliant Luton Town team this season, keep believing and the impossible is possible, never give up. Come on you Hatters!

# Tuesday 5<sup>th</sup> April at 7.45 pm – Peterborough United

Fortunately, the fixture schedule allowed me 8 days' rest after the Hull City adventure, enough time to properly recover and restore my energy levels after my COVID-19 experience. The Peterborough challenge was due to be one of the less demanding challenges, and would be very different to other challenges, mainly due to having some company on the ride. I would be joined by Dave and Luke B from the 'Oh when the town' podcast, which had first been suggested back at the Forest away game when I had met Luke in the pub before the game. However, the planning only really started properly 2 days before the Peterborough trip when we went out for an 18-mile ride to get Luke used to my bike, which he would be using.

This was going to be a huge challenge for Luke, having only ever cycled a third of the distance that we had planned for the Peterborough ride. However, any fears that I had would be put to rest on our pre-ride, which had good elevation, greater than the ratio on the Peterborough ride. The route I planned was slightly longer but less demanding on the elevation.

I was really looking forward to Away Cycle Challenge 22 and excited about having company, as I had cycled alone for the previous 21 challenges. In addition to Luke cycling with me, Dave was the support driver which meant I didn't have to carry extra bags, so I drove to Luke's to drop off the car and prepare for the 64-mile challenge ahead. We set off from Dave's just after 9 am. The plan was to take it nice and steady at Luke's pace with plenty of time for stops and some liquid refreshment.

So, after some interviews and being filmed leaving Dave's, we were on our way from Dunstable, firstly navigating Dunstable traffic through roadworks through to Houghton Regis. The route took us up to Toddington with a slight elevation. This was the first of many similar conversations with Luke, who suggested this was a hill, to which I replied, 'No, it's only an incline!' After a brief stop at Westoning for drinks break, we reached Flitwick at the 10-mile mark, and from there we took the quieter roads through Maulden. The plan was to have our first scheduled stop at Sandy at the 26-mile mark after 2 and a half hours but after a chat and a call to Dave, Luke felt good and we agreed to push on to St Neots where we could have a pub stop for a drink. En route to St Neots, we had to navigate a short distance on the busy A1. Now, I am used to scary sections on busy roads for short periods but was wary whether Luke would be ok with it, so we progressed for what was only a few miles, and we reached St Neots at 35 miles and just over 3 hours of cycling.

It was a welcome break and nice to have a catch-up with Dave and we made another video. The first pint went down well, a new experience for me on my away challenge rides, but it was agreed we would only stay for one as Huntingdon was only 9 miles away where we could have a longer stop and get something to eat. The 9 miles to Huntingdon were flat and an easy section and it seemed that in no time at all, we had arrived in Huntingdon at 44 miles with just over 5 hours of cycling. We found a Wetherspoons and because we had made good progress, we had the luxury of being able to have a 2-hour stop for a few more beers and some food, which was welcomed by us all.

I had got to know Luke and Dave through the podcast and brief chats at the games. Their podcasts had really helped me during my periods of depression, and it had felt like I was in a pub with them, chatting about all things Luton without leaving the comfort zone of my house, so to enjoy their company in a pub environment on a wide range of subjects was a pleasure. We all could have stayed in the pub for much longer, but my leg muscles were starting to tighten, and we still had the final 20 miles to go. It was agreed that Dave would make his way straight to the ground and get parked and we would update him on our progress.

Luke thought the last 20 miles would be a struggle, but he was doing amazingly well considering his limited cycling experience. We were on a countdown, ticking off the miles, and at the 48-mile mark we turned off on a road than ran adjacent to the A1M. It was straight and long and we stayed on this road for 10 miles, and as Luke admitted later, those 10 miles were a struggle, as it is hard to stay focused and push through the miles when there aren't any checkpoints to cross off the list. Although it's not too demanding physically, mentally it can be challenging.

We turned off this section of road at 57 miles, with only 7 miles to go and at 60 miles we reached Yaxley – only 4 miles to go and the end was in sight. We eventually reached the ground to be met by Dave and the other Luke. Away Cycle Challenge 22 had been-achieved, with 64 miles cycled and a moving time cycled of 4 hours 45 minutes with 1,600 feet elevation. Luke was relieved, and it was a fantastic achievement to complete the challenge, which I had really enjoyed.

As is the norm, we first had to take the customary photos and the staff at Peterborough United kindly allowed us all in the ground to have photos taken. After dropping off the bike on the coach, I met Dave and the two Lukes for a pint to recover and look forward to the game. Whilst having a pint in an open-bar tent near the ground, I met quite a few fans who wanted to congratulate me and Luke and a few were generous enough to give me money to donate to the charities. Everyone was so kind and generous, both with their encouragement and donations, although it was amusing that some thought this challenge was easy. I suppose in comparison to others it was.

We made our way to the ground after a drink and took our seats, in a confident mood considering our recent form and Peterborough's league position. Waiting for the game to start, I noticed a missed call from Stu in the media team which I thought was unusual as I didn't need any bags taken. He followed this up with a message to meet him at halftime inside the ground, which left me curious. Anyway, back to the game, we dominated the first half without being threatening, and it appeared we were playing at a higher level with superior movement, pressing and with creativity and surely it was only a matter of time before we scored; however, it stayed 0-0 at halftime.

I met Stu at halftime, who explained that Gary Sweet wanted to speak to me after the game – now I was even more curious.

Soon after the second half started, we deservedly took the lead from super Danny Hylton, with a finish that he has made a career from, finding space in the box from a perfect cross. Now, most of us were expecting the team to press home the advantage and dominate the game for a convincing win; however, this didn't materialize, the chances and possession dried up and Peterborough were more positive and started to create chances. We made a change in bringing on Sonny Bradley for Danny; it appeared that we were trying to protect the lead but after a miss which was easier to score for Peterborough, we conceded 3 minutes before the end and could have lost the game as they hit the post, but we took a point and moved on.

So, I met Gary after the game and he invited me for dinner, a nice touch, and then explained it was at the Grosvenor as I had been nominated for Supporter of the Season. Wow! Just when I think I can't be surprised anymore, this happens. I was told to keep quiet until the announcement a week later. I was buzzing still trying to get my head around it.

It was back on the coach for the journey home, and this time I got off at J11 for the short cycle back to Luke's to collect my car and after a brief chat with Luke, I drove home to finally end a long but enjoyable day completing Away Cycle Challenge 22 and seeing the team get another point nearer the playoffs. Come on you Hatters!

# Monday 11th April 2022 at 7.45 pm – Huddersfield Town

So, after the Peterborough challenge, I had 4 days of recovery before setting off for the 2-day Huddersfield challenge. It should have been only 2 days rest until Sky did their usual thing of moving the game to a Monday night, with zero consideration for supporters and it was Sky who had said during lockdown that football was nothing without supporters. Short memories – anyway, rant over!

Before the Huddersfield trip I had another surprise. A lot of my experiences have left me speechless but when a Luton Town legend and hero of mine, Mick Harford, messaged me and asked if I wanted to meet up for a drink and a chat, it was just unbelievable. I was so excited and nervous at the same time in the days leading up to meeting Mick. So, we met on the Friday, 2 days before I departed for Huddersfield, at a Costa in Harpenden. Mick took the time to meet me and thank me for all my efforts for Prostate Cancer UK as well as supporting the team. He was an absolute gentleman, so humble and down to earth and it was such a privilege to spend a few hours in his company, talking about all things Luton Town, both the current season and the past and also chatting about his battles with prostate cancer as well as talking about me, my challenge and my time as a Luton fan. Mick was genuinely interested in me, which I found hard to believe with my low self-esteem. It was a few hours I didn't want to end and an absolute pleasure. There was a moment where Mick asked someone to take a photo of us and introduced me as a legend. I couldn't quite believe Mick referencing me as a legend. We ended the chat with Mick asking me to come and say hello when I arrived at Huddersfield. On my route home, still buzzing from meeting Mick, I dropped off my bag at the club for my Huddersfield trip and had a nice chat with Dan.

So, back to the preparation for the Huddersfield trip. The change of dates for the fixture meant I had more recovery time, although Peterborough wasn't demanding so I would have preferred a Saturday game and having the Sunday to chill and relax. The nature of having a 2-day challenge with the second day being an evening kickoff is to make the first day the shorter day so as not to have too much waiting time on the day of the game. This is the opposite to a Saturday 3 pm game, although these are becoming rare now at the end of the season.

So, I set off on the Sunday before the game at 9.30 am with a cycle of just under 70 miles to my accommodation in Loughborough. As with a few of the challenge rides that passed through the Leicester region, the route was a familiar one – cycling through Northampton, picking up the A5199 and passing through a number of villages. The road to Wigston was long, straight and uneventful, a road I didn't have to concentrate on too much other than traffic. The weather was pleasant, very different to my cycles on the same route in sub-zero conditions during the winter months. I found some energy and the pace was quicker than normal, between 16 and 17mph, which considering the extra baggage I was carrying was decent for me!

So, after 51 miles and 3 and a quarter hours' cycling, I arrived at Wigston to have my regular stop at Costa for my usual tea, millionnaire shortbread and protein food intake.

I had less than 20 miles to go to for the first day's cycling and navigated my way through Leicester, which for a Sunday afternoon was quite busy, especially with a rugby match taking place. The route took me up the A6 towards Mountsorrel, a busy dual carriageway for a short distance but no surprises for the short ride to Loughborough.

On the later stages of the ride to Loughborough, I noticed that I was struggling to clip my cleats into the pedal on one of the shoes. Now, on the first day's ride this wasn't an issue as there wasn't much elevation, but I knew with 5,000 feet elevation on Day 2, I needed the power to tackle the climbs. Anyway, I had completed Day 1 of Away Cycle Challenge 23, which was 67 miles in just over 4 hours with 2,400 feet elevation. I booked into my accommodation, which was a pub, and with a short walk into town found a pub to get fed and watch some football.

So to say that the start to Day 2 was eventful was an understatement – firstly, not sure if the cleats would last, I searched for a bike shop and eventually found a Halfords which had the cleats. Now, normally the refitting of the cleats is precise and I take my time to fit them, they only have to be out by a fraction to cause discomfort, but I didn't have a lot of time as I had over 80 miles of a hilly cycle ahead of me. Anyway, they were fitted and I was good to go. So, I followed the navigation out of Loughborough on unfamiliar roads – sometimes I become too reliant on the navigation due to my poor sense of direction – and when I arrived in Mountsorrel I realised that I had been cycling in the wrong direction. So, after recalculating, I had actually cycled 11 miles and was still in Loughborough – as if the day hadn't been hard enough, it would be a 90-mile plus day, all part of the challenge!

Eventually, I made my way in the right direction, heading towards Ilkeston in Derbyshire at the 31-mile mark and then heading towards Chesterfield. It's always a challenge navigating cities. – I switch to google maps for city navigations, for better prior warning of road turnings and fewer chances of getting lost. With the issues at the beginning of the day, I had lost the luxury of long breaks but felt I needed a rest to recover and refuel, and at 43 miles at the 3–4-hour point, I stopped at Alfreton for about 20-30 minutes. I still had 50 miles to go and the elevation was about to get harder as I approached the Yorkshire region.

It would be another 13 miles until I reached Chesterfield, where navigating the centre was fairly straightforward, followed by 5 miles of ascents. Nothing brutal but it felt like I was either up or down, with nothing flat. Eventually, it settled down as I approached Sheffield, 12 miles from Chesterfield. Sheffield City Centre was busier and required patience, as I was getting stopped at what seemed like every set of lights. Just when I was wondering where I was, suddenly Sheffield United's ground appeared in my sights and I headed out towards Hillsborough. I had reached Sheffield at the 67-mile mark, with just under 30 miles to go.

I was prepared for more elevation – the clue was the dark green areas on the map. Fatigue was setting in so I was on countdown in 5-mile segments. Penistone was the next landmark to cross off my list and this was achieved at 81 miles. I was nearly at the peak of the climbs, and I had also nearly reached the point where I should have finished so just the extra miles to complete. It is hard not to think about it but just to focus on the finish nearly in sight. Just when I thought I had a flat route into Huddersfield, there was one last climb to finish off a tough day's cycling. Day 2 cycling was completed in 95 miles, nearly 5,000 feet elevation and 6 and a half hours' actual cycling. In total, Away Cycle Challenge 23 was achieved by cycling a total of 162 miles, 10 and a half hours of cycling time and over 7,000 feet of elevation.

In the build-up to the challenge, Huddersfield Town had been supportive, retweeting and sharing details of my challenge. I was met at the ground by Simon, who I had met through a Championship podcast that I had joined. It was great to meet up and after waiting for the Luton team coach to arrive, we went for a drink. It was overwhelming to be approached by so many Huddersfield Town supporters with good wishes – I have said this many times, but the footballing community have really supported me so much. I walked back to the coach with more encouraging support to offload the bike and get ready for the game.

It was a great turnout considering it was a Monday night game, with over 1,000 Hatters fans. We had the better of possession without creating many opportunities with Huddersfield having the better chances and the match went into halftime at 0-0. The game turned around the hour mark with Huddersfield taking the lead, then a well-worked move involving James Bree to win us a penalty. Elijah Adebayo is normally so reliable with penalties but on this occasion failed to find the target and couldn't find an equaliser and the game was over when Huddersfield got a second goal near the end to confine us to a defeat where we could have no complaints about the result.

So, back on the coach for a long journey home. I know it has been a disappointing performance when I struggle to choose a Man of the Match . Anyway, I moved on to Forest at home 4 days later, also on Sky TV. Eventually, several hours later, I got home after a long day but Away Cycle Challenge 23 had been completed.

# Monday 18th April 2022 at 3 pm – Cardiff City

Away Cycle Challenge 24 was across the Easter weekend and I would start after 5 days' rest and recovery from the Huddersfield challenge. The Easter weekend would start with a tense but vital home victory against an in-form promotion rival Nottingham Forest, chosen for Sky TV again. Fortunately, we got a vital 1-0 win to cement our place in the playoffs and put us all in good spirits for the trip to Cardiff City.

The evening before I set off, I had a radio interview with Justin Dealey from Three Counties Radio at 11.30 pm. It is always a pleasure to chat to Justin, and my first interview at the beginning of my challenge had been with him. We chatted about the challenge and finally called it a night ready for the Cardiff challenge.

The long ride into Wales would take a similar route to the one I had experienced on my Swansea ride so I thought I could stay in Chepstow until I found out the same hotel would be nearly 3 times the price I had paid in January. I looked to do most of the distance on the Sunday so planned an overnight stay in Falfield, just 10 miles from the Severn Bridge. So, I set off just after 9.30 am. The forecast was for pleasant, warm temperatures, so I had the luxury of only needing shorts, fingerless gloves, with no thermal layers required and I even packed suncream! I started on a familiar route, as it was my training route through the villages out to Marsh Gibbon towards the Bicester area, where I would pick up the roads to Kirtlington and Witney. I reached Witney at the 50-mile mark in about 3 and a half hours. It was starting to warm up so I took a rest at a coffee shop to recharge my devices and get a pot of tea and cake – this was the halfway mark for the day's cycling.

I followed the familiar route from the Swansea ride although this time I avoided Cirencester, taking the quieter roads and although only having done this part of the route once before, some of the villages I passed through looked familiar. It is surprising that I remembered, as on a lot of the rides I tend to switch off – it is impossible to concentrate 100% as the mind wanders and my thoughts take over whilst trying not to get lost. As the hours passed, the temperature increased, forcing me to take in fluid to avoid becoming dehydrated. You know it's either a warm day or a hard ride when sweat pours into your eyes. Anyway, I made progress to Fairford at the 65-mile mark – it had been 5 hours since leaving home. The Cotswold Waterpark was a landmark I remember and a sign that I had a few hours' cycling left in the day.

The fatigue set in as I counted down the miles in the sunshine. Passing through the counties was an achievement and I saw signs of progress. I knew as I approached Wotton-under-Edge after 6 hours of cycling, that I was near to the end. I approach a 100-mile day in percentages and see the gap between miles cycled against miles to go become greater, just tricks to play on the mind to get through the day's cycling. I arrived at my accommodation just before 5 pm and Day 1 of Away Cycle Challenge 24 had been completed with 102 miles cycled in 6 and a half hours with 3,500 feet elevation climbs. Time to rest up, treat myself to a few ciders and relax.

Day 2 was an early start. With prior knowledge of the ride into Newport, I decided not to have breakfast at the hotel, adding expense for a light breakfast before setting off so I began on an empty stomach, and it was 10 miles until I arrived at the Severn Bridge, stopping for photos, and it was another 5 miles to reach Chepstow. I ignored the cycling app and took the direct road to Newport, which wasn't demanding, and a straight road that I took for the Swansea trip, so it was familiar. At 26 miles I stopped at McDonalds for breakfast. I was less than 20 miles from Cardiff, and whilst enjoying my breakfast, I checked my messages and donation pages to notice an important landmark had been achieved – I had just passed £10,000. I was really emotional and tearful. When I started, I would have been grateful for £1,000 for each charity and £10,000 seemed like an impossible dream. I just kept staring at my screen until I had finished my breakfast. I also had a message to call Les from the Bobbers to confirm I would present an award at the presentation evening, more great news to set me on my way.

4 more miles to Newport and a cycle over the river and I approached a junction for the M4, which looked familiar. I remembered the panic on my Swansea ride trying to avoid joining the M4 by accident! I passed through Castleton at 36 miles towards St Mellons. I was only

5 miles from Cardiff and on the home straight. I encountered traffic which got busier as I arrived in Cardiff, and once again, I noticed familiar sights but this was from my cycle in 2016 around the cricket grounds. It surprises me the random things I remember. I passed Cardiff Castle. The final few miles took an age, being stopped at what seemed like every set of traffic lights, but finally, I could see the ground in the distance and I had completed the 45 miles on Day 2, taking around 3 hours of cycling time.

Away Cycle Challenge 24 had been achieved over 2 days. I had cycled 147 miles in just over 9 and a half hours with 5,000 feet elevation.

On arrival, I met with someone from Cardiff Cty who had messaged me before and was arranging for me to get access to the ground for some photos. Everyone at Cardiff City was so friendly and supportive, and I also met a few well-wishers and Dan from the media team and Simon Pitts and had a catch-up while I waited for the team coach. I also hoped to see James Collins as he had been so supportive of my previous charity venture but unfortunately I didn't see him. When the team arrived, Mick H came over to see me, he always makes time to chat to me, a true legend and a genuine down-to-earth nice, decent guy.

I made my way to the coach and had another surprise in store when I arrived. The Bobbers Travel Club had run a raffle on the coaches and donated the money to my charities, an incredible gesture, they have been so supportive of me and my challenge.

The temperature was comfortable, so I didn't really change, only into my Luton shirt and I made my way into the ground and after getting a pie and chatting in the concourse, I made my way to my seat ready for the game.

The game had a quiet start with few chances created; however, it wasn't long before the injury curse continued – James Shea going off with a bad knee injury which turned out to be a serious injury keeping him out for a long period. Added to that, James Bree collided with the advertising boardings after a late tackle that didn't even warrant a booking and the match got to halftime at 0-0. At this point, with the injuries and down to the minimum, I would have settled for a draw. In the second half we were pressing more with Robert Snodgrass being influential and with 20 minutes to go, a real moment of quality from a Robert Snodgrass cross. Harry Cornick came off the bench to score the winner to send the strong Hatters following into a delight. Harry obviously enjoys 70$^{th}$-minute winners coming off from the bench in Wales, repeating the feat from Swansea. There weren't any dramas and we held on for a vital win and 3 valuable points in our promotion push to send us home happy.

The journey home was uneventful, which couldn't be said for the second coach which broke down and didn't get home until much later.

As is standard for an away southern trip, my journey would end with a cycle home from Flitwick that would start just after 21.15 pm and last just over 45 minutes and at this point, my Cardiff City journey had finally come to an end and it was time to rest and recover before starting work early the next morning, tired but very happy.

With the Fulham game moved to the May bank holiday, Cardiff City would signal the end of April for my challenges. A staggering £1,991 had been donated during the month, taking the total to £10,928, an unbelievable amount. The kindness and generosity from everyone continue to amaze me and is never taken for granted. I am so grateful that the charities are benefitting from my challenge.

# EFL Awards at Grosvenor House Hotel – Sunday 24th April

After the surprising news a month earlier of my nomination for Supporter of the Season, the awards evening came round quite quickly with 4 Championship games to focus on as the playoff push built momentum. My preparation was to arrange the hiring of a suit, and to book accommodation in Paddington. This was going to be an experience that I had never thought would happen in my wildest dreams and I wanted to take it all in. I hadn't really thought about winning the award as just to be nominated was an achievement; however, as the awards event approached, I was really hoping I would win although I didn't prepare a winning speech, as that would be tempting fate.

The day before the awards, we played Blackpool at home in front of the Sky cameras. A hard-fought but disappointing draw despite taking the lead after a few minutes through Elijah, only to concede a penalty and although a draw was a fair result, it could have been different with a late disallowed goal. Anyway, that evening I packed everything for the big day.

We travelled down around lunchtime with suit bags and after navigating a short walk to the hotel check-in, I found a local pub for food and cider before getting ready and arrived at the Grosvenor Hotel for about 6ish, still not believing little me was there to celebrate the EFL season and being nominated too, something I had never imagined when I embarked on my challenge.

After a while we met Mick Harford, Nathan Jones, Gary Sweet, David Wilkinson and Paul Hart. It was surreal to be chatting to them on a social level and not just as a football fan – these were my heroes but when you get to know them, they are just normal people. We all sat down for the meal, and I was loving every moment, taking it all in. The format of the evening was the non-footballing awards were before the team/player awards so I had an idea that the category that I had been nominated for would be quite early in the evening.

As the category was announced my nomination was introduced as a supporter who travelled to away games and hadn't missed a game for a number of years. I bet everyone wondered why I had been nominated. Anyway, I didn't win and although disappointed, I was still proud to be nominated. It was a nice touch that straight after the announcement, Nathan made a point of congratulating me even though I hadn't won. Everyone on the Luton Town table really wanted me to win and had huge respect for my achievement, which meant a lot.

The evening was about celebrating everyone's success on and off the pitch. It was a privilege to be there and a highlight for me was to see Nathan get the Manager of the Season award – just to be there and see him get a deserved acknowledgement for his success with our club was special. The club has come so far, both on and off the pitch, and all the hard work by Nathan, Mick and all the team was being recognised by Nathan's award, the first of many awards in seasons to come.

There were many conversations on the Luton Town table, not all football-related but obviously most of them were. A few of them spring to mind, one being using the truffle board with 11 pieces as a tactic board for the forthcoming Fulham game. I don't think I will have a job on the coaching team!

The other conversation that shocked me was a random comment that I should cycle to Fulham in my suit, to which I replied that I would do so for a significant donation. To my surprise a large donation was agreed; obviously, I wasn't expecting this when I made the suggestion so I was going to enjoy the evening and save the planning of how I was going to fulfil my part of the deal for another day.

The final award of the evening was for the EFL Player of the Season, and it was obvious to everyone that Mitrovic from Fulham would win it and he went up and collected his award and made his speech. Now, as I mentioned before, the evening was a celebration of the season, to recognise unsung heroes as well as achievements on the pitch. Unfortunately, I think Mitrovic thought the evening was all about him and appeared to just turn up for his award and wasn't seen afterwards. There might be other reasons for it but in my eyes it just showed a lack of respect – rant over!

The awards finished and I managed to get a few photos with Mick, Nathan, Gary and David before they left for the evening. They were very complimentary about my achievements, and our club is very lucky to have such brilliant and caring people running it, that genuinely care about everyone at all levels connected with the club.

We wanted to stay and make the most of the evening right until the very end, although we had experienced Grosvenor drinks prices but didn't care, as we didn't want the evening to end. Eventually, we left at approximately 2.30 am and walked back to our hotel. It was about 3.30 am before we got to bed, the end of an incredible evening that I will always remember, and it acts as a reminder to myself when I have moments of low confidence and self-esteem that little old me was nominated for a national football league award for my fundraising efforts.

So, the morning after the night before, we actually felt reasonably good despite the lack of sleep and the alcohol consumed. We checked out and made our way to the tube station en route to Euston and then onwards back home. This was the first opportunity to read all the encouraging messages of congratulations on social media; everyone was genuinely pleased for me and also disappointed that I didn't win, which was incredibly humbling, and I was grateful for all of the support and warmth shown by everyone.

On the journey home, my thoughts turned to the challenge I had agreed to of cycling to Fulham in a suit. Now, obviously, I couldn't cycle in my best suit and I wanted to keep the costs to a minimum so shortly after arriving home just after lunchtime, we spent the afternoon going round charity shops, looking for a suitable suit. First of all we found a Willen Hospice shop in Olney and purchased a pair of trouser for £6, which were perfect, a skinny fit so not baggy trousers, but they would need alterations. We walked around a number of other charity shops in Olney without any success so next we tried Newport Pagnell, where I found a bow tie in one charity shop for £3 and a short-sleeved white shirt, also for £3, in another charity shop. The shirt was perfect – short sleeves for comfort and breathable with the top button done up. I must admit my priorities for buying this suit were completely different to previous suits. Now all I had to do was find a jacket that matched and was comfortable, which proved to be the biggest challenge. I toured charity shops in Woburn Sands, Woburn and various other places before finding a jacket in a Heart Foundation charity shop for £8. I had bought a full suit outfit for £20. The final task was to get the trousers altered – the look on their faces when I turned up to get measured in the trousers wearing cycling shoes, they thought it was a wind-up. So, £26 for the alterations – in total, £46 to dress in a suit for a cycle to Fulham!

My attendance at the EFL awards had had such a positive response and I was receiving regular updates to say that I had received more donations. During April, I had received nearly £2,000 and the donations passed £11,000, an unbelievable amount.

# Monday 2<sup>nd</sup> May 2022 at 5.15 pm – Fulham

So, it came as no surprise that the Fulham game was moved for Sky coverage, with Fulham being promoted to the Premier League, but being moved to the Monday bank holiday was not helpful. The Supporters Trust presentation evening was meant to be on the Sunday before the rearranged game so it had to be rearranged so the players could attend. Also, with the game being played on a Monday, everyone else had played over the weekend. We knew that a positive result would guarantee a playoff place but Fulham, who had already been promoted, would be a tough challenge. Would Nathan rest players for the final game of the season? Would Fulham relax, having already been promoted?

With a Monday fixture, I had all weekend to prepare, and on the Sunday, I went down to the ground for my Prostate PSA test. Throughout my challenge, I had been trying to raise awareness of the importance of men being tested for prostate cancer, so I took the opportunity to take my regular test.

With our playoff place not being assured, I didn't know if Fulham would be the last ride of my challenge but at the beginning, my challenge was to get to Fulham having cycled to all the games/grounds, so I was treating Fulham as the final challenge and I think it was recognised as the final challenge by a lot of people judging by the encouraging messages.

At the end of April, donations had reached £10,928, an unbelievable amount for the 3 charities, and my nomination at the EFL awards the previous weekend had had a positive impact on the donations received. Also, cycling to Fulham in my suit would get a lot of interest.

In the days leading up to the game, Justin Dealey from Three Counties Radio contacted me to say that he wanted to interview me on my arrival at Fulham's ground, which would be fitting as Justin, being a

Luton fan, had given me great support on my challenge and was my first radio interview back in August when I had first started.

So, with the 5.15 pm kickoff, I had the luxury of a lie-in on the morning of the game and I prepared with my usual routine, only this time I swapped my usual cycling attire for my suit. I wasn't sure how comfortable it would be, so I wore cycling shorts under the trousers for extra comfort. I was lucky with the weather for my start and I set off just before 10 am. I was expecting some strange looks!

As with my previous London rides, the start took me on a familiar route through Wing and a number of other villages and I headed out towards the climb up Bison Hill to Whipsnade. After passing the zoo, I stopped to check the suit was in one piece and a guy came over to see if I was ok. He obviously thought I was cycling home after a night out and was shocked to hear of my ride, which was the normal response that I had been expecting for the early part of my ride. After 33 miles and 2 and a quarter hours' cycling, I reached St Albans and carried on towards Elstree, arriving at Edgware an hour later. I was making good progress and wasn't hindered too much by the suit. I was fortunate it was a comfortable 10 celsius degrees, as a warmer day or a rainy day would have made the ride harder wearing the suit.

Due to the close proximity, I was expecting a similar ride to that I had taken to the QPR game, where I'd ended up on a busy dual carriageway in rush hour so I was slightly nervous as I entered London. I passed through Cricklewood and entered the Kensington area, at which point I had been cycling just over 4 hours but when I entered Hammersmith, I knew that I wasn't too far away, only a few miles to go. I made a call to Justin so he could meet me arriving at the ground, but unfortunately he was delayed so I arrived getting more strange looks. I did eventually meet up with Dan and Stu with my bag whilst I waited for Justin.

Eventually, Justin arrived, and he interviewed me with a band playing in the background. I enjoy my interviews with Justin, he always makes me feel relaxed and it's like chatting to a mate down the pub about football rather than a radio interview. With the interview completed, I waited for the team coach to see the players, where I was acknowledged by a few. Mick always makes a point of coming over to chat and even Harry commented on my suit looking good. Now, with Harry being known for his dress sense, it was quite a compliment for him to comment on the suit.

I then made my way to find the coach which, at Fulham, is always parked on the main road away from the ground. I loaded the bike on the coach, and I decided to stay in the suit for the duration of the game. I was easily recognised and received encouraging comments as I had a well-earned cider in the ground.

Now, as far as the game was concerned, I was treating it as a free hit, thinking if our goal difference wasn't affected too much and we didn't get any injuries, we still had our playoff aspirations in our own hands and an outside chance we could guarantee it with a game to go. My hopes for an injury-free game did not start well with Allan Campbell injured in the warm-up. The first 20 minutes were encouraging, as we competed with their highly paid stars, then we conceded just before the half-hour mark and that opened the floodgates.

Now, I know the game wouldn't define our season, but as the goals went in on a regular basis – 3,4,5 then 6 with still 12 minutes to go – it was embarrassing being taunted by Fulham fans, and we eventually lost 7-0. We all made our way out of the ground while they celebrated becoming champions. I won't miss not going back, although at that time, there was still a possibility if we got promoted.

I didn't realise until later on the coach, just how many donations that I had received on the day. In total, over the weekend, I received in excess of 80 donations, totalling nearly £1,000, which was absolutely staggering and took my total over £11,000.

So, as with my southern games, I had the final cycle home after I left the coach just before 9.30 pm because of the late kickoff. I changed out of the suit for the final journey home, which took 45 minutes and got home just before 10.30 pm.

So, because of the Fulham result, I wouldn't know if this would be my final away cycle challenge of the season. We had a nervous home game against Reading in 5 days to determine if we would make the playoffs and have at least one more away cycle. So, before the season-defining game, I had the chance of a few days' rest and reflection on making it to the final regular away cycle challenge. Come on you Hatters!

# A celebration of the season's achievements

So, before the season's celebrations could take place, there was the matter of the regular season being completed and specifically, a playoff place to be secured. Going into the last game of the season at home to Reading, we sat in 6$^{th}$ place, the final playoff place, but potentially could be caught by Middlesbrough or Millwall so although winning a secure playoff place sounded easy, I was feeling extremely nervous.

Before the game, the club made a really nice gesture by having me interviewed on the pitch by Darren and then I had a walk around the pitch, a really emotional experience, seeing everyone standing to applause. I was trying to take it all in and it was an experience I will never forget. As I walked in front of the Kenilworth, I heard a cry of 'There's only one Mark Crowther' and I looked up to see Gary from the Bobbers Travel Club. I never thought I would hear that sung from the Kenilworth!

Anyway, back to the game. It was an incredible atmosphere, with everyone getting behind the team and with one eye on the other key games. We were comfortable at 0-0 and other results going in our favour and it looked like we were going into halftime at 0-0 until a goalkeeping error allowed Harry Cornick to score and give us some breathing space. There were no further goals but we had secured our playoff place, an unbelievable achievement, all things considered, and we celebrated after the game and looked forward to a 2-leg play off against Huddersfield Town, so another cycle to Huddersfield to plan. Come on you Hatters!

The Supporters Trust presentation evening is a great chance to celebrate both the clubs' and players' achievements and for the supporters to mix with the players. They are always well-supported, and the players always make time for the fans, and are friendly and approachable and this year was no exception. It had been a few years since the previous presentation evening due to COVID-19 so I was looking forward to it.

We arrived quite early and were met on our way in by Simon Pitts, who always hosts the evening and does a brilliant job. First thing was to see the table plan, then get a drink and meet everyone. I knew a lot more people than at previous presentation evenings through my challenge event. Now, ahead of the evening, through a Bobbers Travel club raffle, I knew that I was presenting an award, So, everyone took their seat including the players joining their respective tables and I was pleased to see that Harry Cornick was on our table, at which point the evening began.

So, the first award was the Away Player of the Season (voted for by supporters of the Bobbers Travel Club) which I was presenting, and I went on stage where Simon introduced me as the cyclist travelling to all the games and after a brief introduction, I presented the trophy to Allan Campbell, which was thoroughly well-deserved. Now, I had presumed this would be the last time that I would have to speak in front of the several hundred people attending, how wrong I was.

The second award was the 'Contribution to Luton Town' award and Tony Murray, who was presenting it, mentioned that the winner has just been on stage. I still didn't realise it was me until my name was called out, and to say that I was genuinely shocked was an understatement. As I wasn't expecting an award, I hadn't prepared a speech so after being presented with the award, I just spoke from the heart, talking about why I'd done the challenge and why the charities were so important to me. I then started to talk about my struggles with my mental health prior to this challenge, and I felt myself becoming more emotional and, on several occasions, I had to stop to compose myself. I was looking out at everyone who was in silence listening to my speech as I held back the tears to finish. Then, incredibly, as I finished my speech and handed the microphone back to Simon, I could see everyone get out of their seats to give me a standing ovation, an incredible moment that will stay with me forever. I made my way back to my seat to high fives from Harry and Robert Snodgrass on the next table.

There was a few more awards given out before a break for a buffet meal and whilst queuing for food, I was surprised again to have players come up to me to shake my hand and congratulate me – first Peter Kioso, then Gabriel Osho and Elliot Thorpe. This was a surreal moment to receive praise from my heroes. The awards evening continued with Allan Campbell and Kal Naismith picking up most of the awards with Kal Naismith receiving 'Player of the Season'. There was then a photo with all the award winners, and to my surprise again, I was asked to go up on stage for the photo, another surreal moment.

I managed to chat with a number of people after the awards. Everyone was so nice and genuinely happy for me to receive the award and I also had a chat with a number of the players and had photos taken and they were all very complimentary about both my speech and my achievement. This meant so much to me and was definitely something I hadn't expected, both when I started my challenge and also when I arrived for the evening. It had been a brilliant evening and we were the last to leave before making our way home.

Due to the rescheduled Supporters Trust presentation evening, it meant that the Sponsors celebration evening was just 2 days later, which I attended for the first time. It was different to the Supporters Trust evening but a similar format to the Christmas dinner evening. Unlike the Christmas dinner, which had been on the evening before I set off for Blackpool, I had a few days' rest and relaxation before the playoff weekend games, leaving on the Sunday for the 2-day trip to Huddersfield.

Prior to the commencement of the evening, the players mixed with the supporters around the bar and it was a nice that the players recognised and acknowledged me. I had a nice chat with Elliot Thorpe and Jordan Clark – even after a season of compliments, they still come as a surprise to me, especially when I receive them from the players – just to get their acknowledgement with a high five, handshake or just a nod made me smile in amazement.

I was on the table with Stewart and a number of people from the Bobbers Travel Club, which was nice, and the proceedings started while the food was brought out. The evening started with multiple choice game to win a cash prize followed by player interviews on the stage and it was really interesting to hear from Nathan talking in detail about his coaching team and the vision for the club – it made you proud to support this great club and lucky that we have so many brilliant people who make key decisions that are driving the club forward. During the breaks between meal courses, it was another opportunity to chat to some of the players and I really enjoyed chatting to Tom Lockyer, Reece Burke and Gabriel Osho, who are all so grounded, humble, down-to-earth and approachable. The main part of the event ended with an auction, and it always shocks me the amount of money raised for the memorabilia, but it is for great causes.

The evening was also a good opportunity to catch up with people that I had got to know through my challenge – specifically, Neil and Yvonne, who kindly invited me as a hospitality guest to the Bristol City game and also Dave, Luke Buttaro and Luke from 'Oh when the town' podcast, who have been so supportive of my challenge and their podcast was a great help to me in lockdown when I was struggling with depression.

Obviously, much of the chat was about the playoffs and everyone was positive and excited at the opportunity of getting promoted. The players had to leave early and, on their way out, it was such a nice gesture from Jordan Clark to make a point of wishing me good luck for my ride to Huddersfield. I was one of the last to leave and as I had work the next day, the holiday leave that I had had to take for my challenge meant I didn't have the luxury of a extra day off. I booked a taxi home, so it was after 2 am before I got to bed, tired but happy at a brilliant evening and excited and nervous for the playoffs with the home leg just 3 days away. Come on you Hatters!

# Monday 16th May at 7.45PM – Huddersfield Town – Playoff Semi Final 2nd Leg

After recovering from the end of season evenings, I prepared for the weekend's playoffs and my second cycle to Huddersfield Town. The preparation for the ride included a few rides, which were easy, low-intensity and high-cadence indoor rides just to keep my legs ticking over, and they helped me to control the intensity and the cadence. Wednesday was 1 hour of Vo2 max development-controlling level of intensity intervals and Thursday was a threshold pyramid session, which was fun and also like a game to manage threshold interval levels. I had decided to take a more demanding but more enjoyable (I think that is how you describe it!) route to Huddersfield. With Friday being the first leg of the playoffs and not being able to focus on anything else, Friday was a rest day with Saturday a steady 20-mile ride after dropping off the car at Barbara and David's for my final northern cycle of the challenge.

So, Friday was a big day for the first leg of the playoffs. The 2 regular season games against Huddersfield Town were tight, hard-fought, competitive games which we had drawn at home 0-0 and lost away a few weeks before at 0-2. I was expecting the playoff games to be similar.

It was a great atmosphere as you would expect from our home game and we started on the front foot with positive intent. However, we got caught on the break and went behind in the 12th minute, not the perfect start but we kept pressing and got a deserved equalizer after half an hour from Sonny Bradley, who does love a goal in front of the Sky cameras. Both teams had strong claims for penalties not given so went in at halftime 1-1. In the second half we struggled to make an impact, Huddersfield dominated possession without creating clear-cut chances. Maybe the tiredness had taken its toll and we'd lost the cutting edge but we remained competitive without creating any opportunities and the match finished 1-1. I was happy with a draw going into the second leg and think both sides would take the positives from the first leg, a quick turnaround before the second leg on Monday evening.

After dropping off the car on the Saturday, the rest of the day was spent preparing for my 2-day cycle to Huddersfield, checking my bike and packing – when I say packing, my usual routine is to get everything out, leave it all over the lounge and pack late evening or early morning so I don't forget anything. It usually involves several attempts at checking and re-checking. It didn't help that the weather forecast was mixed so I had to prepare for different conditions – it was forecast to rain, but the day started cloudy but dry and 10-12 degrees.

Regarding the route, the plan was to cycle 100 miles on the Sunday and depending how I felt, this would determine the route on the Monday. I hoped to take the harder route if I felt ok.

I set off at 9.30 am, and my phone was busy with a lot of encouraging messages of support, messages which have always helped me on my long 2-day cycles. It can be quite lonely as I cross off the checkpoints and miles so the distraction of messages is a great source of motivation and also the fact that so many people are supporting me.

The route started on a familiar route out through Milton Keynes, through Hanslope and a number of other villages, bypassing Northampton and reaching Duston at the 25-mile mark, having been cycling for just over one and a half hours, so this was one quarter of the distance for the day completed, another landmark to tick off. If it was going well, I would cross off a quarter, a third, half, three-quarter distances etc. , If I'm having a bad time then I tick off 5-mile intervals but this was a good ride so far. The second quarter took me on more familiar routes towards Lutterworth, which I reached at the 47-mile mark, having been cycling for just over 3 hours. I was nearly at the halfway mark for the day. The weather had stayed dry, a cloudy day but mild at around 12 to 15 degrees.

At this point, I started to feel tiredness in my legs and looked for a coffee shop and at 60 miles I passed through Desford to find somewhere to stop. I had broken the back of the day's cycling and the stop was as much to recharge my Garmin and phone as it was to rest my legs and refuel with protein bars and some treats as a reward. After a 30- minute break, the elevation difficulty increased just after my stop for about 10 miles as I cycled into Derbyshire, so I was grateful for the rest and I carried on through Coalville at 69 miles, with only about 30 miles to go for the day. It flattened off as I approached the Alvaston area and although I wasn't sure of my exact locations, signs to Pride Park gave it away. The route avoided the centre of Derby and at this point I only had 12 miles to go, and it wasn't too demanding for the rest of the day's cycling.

I finally arrived at my accommodation just after 5 pm, having completed Day 1 of my Away Cycle Challenge 26, having cycled 100 miles in just over 6 hours with 4,000-feet elevation climbs, although I did have to do an additional 0.7 miles to reach another century ride. The accommodation at the Hurt Arms in a place called Ambergate was perfect for a night's relaxation and a chance to refuel and also catch up on the messages and generosity from everyone as the donations had been coming in during my day's cycling.

As I relaxed and contemplated Day 2, my dilemma was the route I would take. Fortunately, I managed to stay dry, and the rain waited until during the night. I had broken the back of the journey and had only 60 miles to go with all day to get there so I decided to take a route through the Peak District – lovely views but some tough climbs ahead of me.

Day 2 started just before 10 am with some brutal climbs to wake up my legs in some light rain, which was a sign of how hard the day would be. The elevation eventually levelled out and I reached Minster at 11 miles, and then headed into the heart of the Peak District and reached Bakewell at 17 miles. This had taken me nearly an hour and a half due to difficulties and, wanting to have made significant progress before I stopped, I carried on. Cycling in the Peak District wasn't a complete surprise as I had had a few weekends there so some of the route was familiar. At the 26-mile mark, and having cycled for 2 hours, nearly halfway for the day, I reached Hathersage. I hadn't had a proper breakfast before leaving so after 2 hours of challenging climbs, I started to fatigue and decided a rest and refuel was much needed so found a place to stop to get fed, warm up and charge my devices.

The views and scenery were stunning. I don't think my legs appreciated it though! I had reached a place called Midhopestones that I remember and I was making my way towards Penistone. I recalled a brutal climb before Penistone but thought I had escaped it – unfortunately not. It took all my efforts just to turn the pedals but I managed it and arrived at Penistone at the 47-mile mark – only 13 miles to go but at this point, my gears developed a fault and kept slipping gears and moving rings – even the bike was complaining. Luckily, the worst of the climbs were over, but I had to nurse the gears to the end, occasionally stopping when the chain came off. 52 miles was the start of the descent towards Huddersfield, and I eventually arrived at the John Smith Stadium to complete my Away Cycle Challenge 26. The Day 2 cycle was 60 miles of cycling for nearly 5 hours with a brutal 5,700 feet of elevation. To put it into perspective, the previous day had been 100 miles and 4,000-feet climbs. Overall, the 2-day challenge was 160 miles, over 9,000 feet of elevation and nearly 11 hours of cycling.

After arriving, I had some time to pass and found a pub a short distance away to get a well-deserved pint before making my way back to the ground, where Justin Dealey from Three Counties Radio wanted to interview me again and we had a nice chat about the ride and the important playoff second leg. Fortunately, I had avoided the heavy rain all day and then while at the ground the heavens opened, but at least it was after I arrived. Shortly after, the team coach arrived and several of the players: Mick, Jordan Clark, Harry Cornick and Elijah came over to see me, which was such a nice gesture when they were focused on the game. It was amusing shortly after that someone asked who I was and if I was I famous, as the players were coming over to see me!

After making my way to the coach to offload my broken bike and to get changed, I made my way into the ground for the massive game ahead.

Like the first leg we started positively, pressing. Movement and passing were good and we took the game to Huddersfield and were dominating the first half, creating chances. Unfortunately, we weren't able to take the lead that we deserved on the clear-cut chances created, and the game could have been out of sight. I was really happy and proud how we were playing and hoped we could convert the chances. We went in at half-time 0-0, hoping we wouldn't be punished for the missed opportunities.

The second half was more even as Huddersfield came more into the game but we were still competitive and as the game moved into the last 15 minutes we hoped a moment of brilliance could win us the game or at the very least take it into extra time. Unfortunately, Huddersfield got the crucial goal after 82 minutes and as much as we tried we didn't trouble their keeper. The ref blew for fulltime and the dream for this season was over. When we have better numbers in all of the attacking stats away from home in such a crucial game, it shows how well we played, we just didn't take our opportunities.

I was feeling gutted but proud of the performance, not just during this game but over the whole season. It had been an incredible season that we will always remember and for myself, unbelievable experiences to treasure. However, the actions of a minority of idiot Huddersfield fans during the pitch invasion with Jordan Clark, Nathan Jones and maybe others being abused, were disappointing, totally unnecessary and disrespectful. It meant that the players couldn't come over to thank us all and for us to show our appreciation for their efforts. The pitch invasion wasn't an isolated incident and would be repeated across most of the playoff games.

We made our way back on the coaches and made our way home. As well as being gutted at the result, it also dawned on me that my away cycle challenge was finally over. I had received just over £400 in donations over the weekend of the playoffs and donations had passed £13,500, an incredible amount donated by everyone and I was extremely -grateful and proud.

# Mad Hatter Away Cycle Challenge Achieved

The morning after the playoff defeat, which signalled the end of a memorable season and also the completion of my away cycle challenge, was a period of reflection on both the football and the challenge. There was so much to be proud of and so many memories to take away, and when it didn't end in the way we had all hoped, usually there is immense disappointment and regret. How could it have ended differently? And although we were all gutted, when we all look back, to even finish sixth and qualify for the playoffs was a massive achievement.

If you asked every Luton Town fan, even the most optimistic fan, they probably wouldn't dare to dream of a chance to get promotion, and you look at some of the teams that didn't make the playoffs – the size of the clubs, the money spent chasing the supposed promised land, the risks taken, the sacking of managers for unrealistic targets not achieved – when you compare this to how our brilliant club is run, the superb structure right from the very top through to the playing staff, brilliantly run by Nathan, his team and the players, down to the supporters, everyone plays their part, the decisions are made by everyone with the very best intentions of making the club develop and grow and everyone should be very proud of their achievements. Everyone you come into contact with, either behind the scenes or on match days, and the players are all so friendly, supportive, kind and warm. In my opinion, this is due to the culture created by the club, the integrity and everyone being a valued part of the success – there are no superstars. An acronym that holds true is TEAM – Together Everyone Achieves More.

There is definitely no one at the club that feels we have reached the summit this season. We are on a journey heading in the right direction as we have been for the last 10 years or so since 2020 came on board with their vision of what can be achieved. In November 2022, Rob Edwards became the clubs new manager after the departure of Nathan Jones and is a great appointment, Rob is aligned to the clubs progression and ambitions and understands the club's values. I was fortunate to chat with Rob at the Christmas dinner and after a few minutes conversation it was clear Rob will be a great success to create the next chapter in the clubs history.Come on you Hatters!

Regarding my away cycle challenge, after the wheels stopped turning as I arrived at Huddersfield and, as it turned out with the defeat, the challenge had come to an end. Across 10 months, 26 away challenges, 2,970 miles cycled, 202 hours of cycling time, 127,343 feet elevation and 87,375 calories burned, of course this challenge was much more than these numbers.

On reflection, and thinking back to my own wellbeing when I came up with the idea 18 months previously at a time when I was not in a good place and struggling to cope with the most basic of functions and even leaving the house was a massive challenge, looking back, this challenge has never just been about me but has helped me to take the focus away from me and focus on supporting charities I feel passionately about. This challenge has been my life for 18 months, from planning the rides, accommodation, training, giving support to the charities to raising awareness and donations through interaction with everyone, both face to face and on social media. As you probably know, if you have come into contact with me, the compliments I've received never come easy to me through my lack of self-esteem, low self-confidence and low self-worth but over the season I have learned to accept and embrace them more and one area that has surprised me, bearing in mind where I have come from 18 month to 2 years ago, is how I have grown into the exposure the event has given me. I certainly wouldn't have believed that I would be doing live radio and TV interviews from where I was.

As I have mentioned, this challenge wasn't about me, it was following my passion for Luton Town and cycling to raise awareness and donations for these three incredible charities: Keech Hospice, Prostate Cancer UK and CALM (Campaign Against Living Miserably), for the staff and volunteers who work tirelessly trying to make people's lives better and for the people and their families and friends whose lives have been affected. You are all the real heroes and have been my inspiration to keep going. There have been times I have been wet, cold, tired, lost or sometimes all at once but this pales into insignificance in comparison to the challenges you have all faced and

I have been so proud to make a very small contribution in helping to raise awareness and the incredible amount everyone has donated.

On the subject of donations, they were still coming in long after the Huddersfield game. I had been running a competition to win a signed shirt generously donated by the club, by guessing the calories burned on my season-long challenge and in the hope that we would reach the playoff final. I set the closing date of 30th May. As the date passed and I announced the lucky winner, I was amazed that an unbelievable amount of £3,413 had been donated just in the month of May.

On the 7th June, I announced on social media that the final amount raised was an unbelievable £15,781 and shortly afterwards, the football club shared it on the website which was a really nice way to announce the end of the challenge.

This has been my fifth charity cycle challenge since 2016, raising donations and awareness for great causes and in total, I have raised £24,000. This has been, by far, the most satisfying and enjoyable challenge.

I think back to the beginning of the challenge and my expectations for the season. Obviously, I hoped to finish, but if I raised £1,000 for each charity then I would have been satisfied. I remember a conversation with Gary outside Birmingham City in mid-February after my 17$^{th}$ challenge when donations had just passed £8,000 and he predicted that I would double the amount. Unbelievably, he was right. The challenge wouldn't have been the success it has been, without the unbelievable generosity of everyone that has donated to the 3 brilliant charities, so a heart felt thank you to everyone one of you. It is difficult to find the words to express my gratitude.

I think of the memories that will stay with me forever and something that I didn't account for at the beginning of the challenge were the friendships I have made over the season, people who will hopefully remain friends for many years to come. Your friendship, support and encouragement has meant everything to me, more than you can possibly realise, so thank you!

So many people have contributed to my challenge being a success. Just to name a few, to Stewart, Les, John and everyone from the Bobbers Travel Club, without your support to get me and my bike home after every game, the challenge wouldn't have been possible.

To everyone at Luton Town Football Club, especially Stu and Dan, thank you! Nothing was ever too much trouble and without your help (especially in the winter!) I really don't know how I would have coped, and to Gary, David, I have been blown away by the warmth and support you showed me, thank you! To Mick Harford – wow, what a legend, it has been a pleasure to get to know you in person and I have been proud to support Prostate Cancer UK.

To Justin, Chris, Toby and everyone at Three Counties Radio, you have always given me the opportunity to promote my challenge, you have been a great help, so thank you.

A huge thank you to Barbara and David, who looked after my car for the duration of the long away trips to avoid additional cycling home late at night after the northern games.

Finally, thank you kate, for your support, encouraging me during the challenging moments and being one of my biggest supporters.

Of course, it would be impossible to thank everyone and apologies if I haven't mentioned you, but you know who you are and how much your support has meant to me.

Just when I thought there wouldn't be any more surprises, I received a call from Toby at Three Counties Radio to tell me that I had been nominated by Keech Hospice for a fundraising award at the Make a Difference awards hosted by Three Counties Radio, another unexpected surprise. Ahead of the awards I met Toby at Keech Hospice to meet some of the team, have some action shots taken and make a recording to be aired on Three Counties Radio to promote the awards evening. It was also a great opportunity to meet Melissa and some of the team at Keech, who all do such incredible work. Although it would be nice to win an award, just to be nominated is an amazing feeling and recognition of my challenge but also recognition for the unbelievable generosity from everyone to raise such an unbelievable amount for the charities. The awards take place in September and although I didn't win the award, just being recognised was a brilliant achievement.

So, what does the future hold? The weeks after the season and the challenge have left a huge void as it's impossible not to have feelings of an anti-climax and thoughts of 'what next?' and by the time you read this book, the new season will be well underway, and I will enjoy next season travelling by more conventional methods of transport which will take a few games to adjust.

I remain positive for the future, and I recognise more than ever the importance of talking during difficult times, and not being afraid to ask for help, or reaching out for anyone that is struggling. Everyone deserves happiness in their lives. At the time of writing, I am planning my next football cycle challenge, cycling to 116 football clubs in the Premiership, Championship, Leagues 1 & 2 and the National league for deserving causes in April & May 2023, I am positive that it will be a great experience and more importantly raise a lot of donations.

If you have made it to the end of my first book, thank you. I hope you found it as enjoyable as my first experience of writing has been and that it has given you an insight into my thoughts, feelings and emotions throughout the experience.

Mad Hatter Mark

COYH